WIN ♥ LOSE ♠ OR ♣ DRAW?

Gambling with America's Small Towns

Patrick Long, Jo Clark and Derek Liston

College of Business and Administration
University of Colorado at Boulder

The Aspen Institute
Rural Economic Policy Program

ISBN: 0-89843-161-1

Table of Contents

List of Figures

Preface

Gambling, as an economic and social force in the United States, has grown enormously over the past ten years, and it likely will continue to do so through the end of this century. As we look toward the millennium and beyond, we cannot ignore the political, economic and moral controversies that seem to arise naturally around gambling. In order to ensure the orderly growth and development of gambling in this country, community leaders and state policymakers must face these controversies head on, taking a proactive role in determining the direction gambling will take. They must consider carefully the changing social values, the political intricacies and the economic arguments that fuel the debate in this ever-widening gambling arena.

Win ♥ Lose ♠ or ♣ Draw? Gambling with America's Small Towns is an important pioneering effort to uncover some of the key policy issues of small town gambling in the 1990s. Based upon their comprehensive study of small town gambling in Colorado and South Dakota, the authors present us with a broad spectrum of issues and pose the many questions we should be asking ourselves. The authors acquaint policymakers with the facts. At the same time, they appeal to policymakers to carefully examine the issues, to identify possible courses of action for addressing this upsurge in gambling, and to create guidelines for lawmakers and community leaders to use in planning for the future.

Win ♥ Lose ♠ or ♣ Draw? Gambling with America's Small Towns is an important pioneering effort to uncover some of the key policy issues of small town gambling in the 1990s

To my knowledge, no other document has been written that so exhaustively analyzes the impact of gambling and lays out the implications of gambling activity for states and local communities. This investigation clearly challenges lawmakers across the country to take action. The authors warn us that developing a policy for small town gambling, given the current social milieu, is difficult. State policymakers simply are not experienced in making decisions about gambling. Gambling doesn't seem to fit the normal patterns of other state economic development activities, and gambling behavior doesn't fit the normal patterns associated with other leisure time activities.

Fortunately, with the information the authors present in this book, the reader has the valuable data and insight needed to untangle the complexities of small town gambling. The conceptual tools provided here most certainly will enable lawmakers and community leaders to develop sound policy guidelines that will set a positive direction for years to come.

Dr. David Edgell
Director
Office of Policy and Planning
United States Travel and Tourism Administration
U.S. Department of Commerce

Executive Summary

Revenues from gambling appear to be so great that many small towns now look at gambling as a solution to their economic troubles. The challenges that states and communities face in initiating gambling in rural areas are substantial. Many policymakers, well aware that the gambling industry is volatile and their potential for error is great, are seeking guidance on how to proceed.

It is not just the volume of gambling activity that makes state policy important. It's also the broad-reaching effects that the decision to approve gambling has on a state's people and governmental capacity. Indeed, the experience of states and communities that already are dealing with gambling can best be described as a mixed bag, poorly understood in economic, social and political terms.

Policymakers, well aware that the gambling industry is volatile and their potential for error is great, are seeking guidance on how to proceed

The South Dakota and Colorado Experiences

Gambling is appearing across the country in a variety of forms. Deadwood, South Dakota, and Black Hawk, Central City and Cripple Creek, Colorado, have implemented one of these forms—community-based, limited-stakes casino gambling—with varying degrees of success. Based on data collection, a residential survey, leadership interviews and focus groups conducted in 1992 and 1993, the experiences of these small mountain towns make it clear that gambling has the potential both to offer significant benefits and to generate serious costs. And, as might be expected, the communities' decisions to permit gambling have forced them to make economic and social tradeoffs, many of which were difficult to anticipate.

South Dakota and Colorado have approached the implementation of gambling differently, with different results. South Dakota limits the number of gambling devices allowed by gambling establishment, Colorado by percentage of space. South Dakota has maintained a consistent state tax rate since it initiated gambling; Colorado has adjusted its tax rate each year. South Dakota allocates a majority of gambling tax revenues and license and application fees to historic restoration and preservation, defined broadly to include streets, water, sewer and low-interest loan programs for both commercial and residential property. Colorado defines historic preservation more narrowly and allocates a much smaller portion of state tax revenues for that purpose in the gambling towns.

Each of these gambling communities has experienced rapid and dramatic growth and change—in its economy, civic life and culture

Deadwood, South Dakota, differs from the Colorado towns because it is a larger community both physically and by population, is less geographically constrained, has a more diversified economy, and provides more basic community services. In addition, Deadwood offers visitors more local tourism attractions and accommodations and has two additional years of experience with gambling. Nonetheless, each of these gambling communities has experienced rapid and dramatic growth and change—in its economy, civic life and culture. Among the clearest indicators of change are:

♦ Commercial property values have skyrocketed, along with the demands on the physical and social infrastructure.

♦ Both entertainment and restaurant establishments have increased in number, while shopping outlets for retail and basic supplies have dwindled to the point of scarcity in some gambling communities, and have disappeared altogether in others.

♦ Local residents feel they have lost much of their political influence, and that the gambling industry now has the ear of the politicians.

♦ Noise, traffic, congestion and an influx of the "new" gambling tourists have replaced the relative peace and tranquility that once blanketed the towns.

♦ Local gathering places have been supplanted by casinos.

♦ Parking—both for residents and visitors—has become a major problem.

- Many residents claim that their community is no longer an ideal place to live and would consider moving.

- Few residents recommend that other communities consider legalizing gambling.

In short, the first communities to implement limited-stakes casino gambling have experienced what might best be referred to as "a revolution, not an evolution."

Although voters in South Dakota and Colorado have approved legalized gambling, state officials view the industry as "different" than other economic diversification strategies—and they treat it as such. Indeed, gambling industry officials in both states expressed concern that they have no political voice; that they are operating in an unstable and unpredictable tax, regulatory and policy environment; and that they generally are not appreciated for their economic and civic contributions to the community.

State officials view the industry as "different" than other economic diversification strategies —and they treat it as such

Community planning in South Dakota and Colorado around the influx of gambling has, for the most part, been reactive rather than proactive. This stems from the lack of available financial and technical resources, the inability to accurately predict the competition for investment in (and, thus, the scale of) gambling development, a general lack of experience with rural community gambling, and perhaps an unwillingness among commercial property owners, local residents and government officials to look beyond gambling's promise of economic gain at its potential to create civic and economic costs.

Current Policy Practice

Because too few states yet have any lengthy experience, it is premature to identify definitive "best practices" that can guide states in their efforts to successfully establish limited-stakes casino gambling. Nonetheless, the recent experience of South Dakota and Colorado and the findings from a survey of other states that offer non-tribal casino gambling provide some early indications of how state policy can influence the success of rural community gambling initiatives.

States need to balance regulatory firmness with policies that maintain a viable gambling industry

Regulation. Perhaps because it is the most straightforward and comfortable for them, most states emphasize their role as a gambling *regulator* above all others. Experience indicates, however, that states need to balance regulatory firmness with policies that help maintain a viable gambling industry. Regulations (or taxation levels) that are too onerous not only can weaken the casino operations or drive them to other locations, they may in fact create some of the problems they are designed to avoid.

Revenue Collection and Distribution. Closely tied to regulation are the collection and distribution of gambling revenues, that is, how much—and how—gambling proceeds are taken in and reallocated by the relevant government jurisdictions. At least four levels of government are involved and affected—cities, counties, schools and the state—but no state in the survey has built all four into the revenue process. The state typically plays the largest role in collecting revenues, while cities or towns generally collect fewer dollars via device fees, parking fees and riverboat boarding fees. Counties and schools usually depend on indirect revenue gains through property value increases for their share of money distributed by the state.

The question of who benefits from the distribution of revenues created by gambling is an important one and deserves thoughtful design. To ensure that all residents benefit, many recommend that gambling tax revenues be used to fund quality of life improvements for the entire community—improved streets, water and sewer; better social services; recreation centers, new parks, senior services, community festivals and similar purposes.

Economic Development Assistance. Once a statewide vote or a legislative initiative legalizes gambling, it becomes a legitimate business. Thus, the types and levels of state technical and financial support available for economic development can also affect the success of gambling. But gambling seems different than "regular" business.

Although both states and communities may envision gambling as an economic gold mine, it is also viewed with moral apprehension. Consequently, even though most states offer programs to attract and benefit new industry—tax breaks, special zoning, training programs, inclusion of industry officials on civic boards, assistance with bonding, marketing help, and a host of others— considerably less state business development assistance is made available to firms in the gambling industry.

Social Impacts. Perhaps the most difficult and least resolved set of issues relative to the introduction of gambling in small communities relates to the social consequences. Although existing evidence points to significant social consequences, most states interviewed simply prefer to look the other way and have elected not to address them. By contrast, during the energy boom of the 1970s, oil-rich states in the West that grew by leaps and bounds often created community impact assistance funds, provided state credit for infrastructure bonding, initiated worker training programs, offered grant-writing and other technical assistance, established social programs for alcohol and other kinds of abuse, set up special programs for the children of construction workers, established formulas for revenue sharing for impacted areas, and in general, were strong advocates of the affected communities.

The resident survey conducted in the gambling communities revealed the need for similar assistance. If gambling is being introduced into very small towns, it is totally unrealistic to think the community has the resources and wherewithal to cope with the initial variety and scale of impacts likely to occur. To limit or deny state assistance in these cases abandons not only the community but the gambling industry, which is making significant investments. Such a hands-off policy also neglects the needs of tourists, who comprise a substantial economic market for many states, and who will judge whether to return based on their experience.

Although both states and communities may envision gambling as an economic gold mine, it is also viewed with moral apprehension

Planning for Gambling

Experience is accumulating rapidly on both the pros and cons of gambling, as well as on strategies that deal with gambling in various situations. It's clear that few areas that currently allow gambling started out with a well-conceived vision about what they wanted gambling to look like, and then implemented the right set of policy enablers and controls to achieve it. What all the complexity with regulation, revenues, economic development and social impacts suggests is that planning is essential at the community, state and industry levels. And such planning should start early, when bringing the industry in is at the concept stage.

During a gambling initiative campaign, or once gambling is permitted and in the planning stages, states can find and provide information to help local communities work through the many decisions that must be made. They also can offer technical assistance to help address the wide range of inescapable questions dealing with the scale of the gambling industry, the extent of the competition and who should benefit:

States must recognize that the gambling industry itself is undergoing fundamental change

♥ **Set scale.** Decisions on appropriate scale tend to be influenced most by the social, environmental and economic "carrying capacity" of the geographic area. Carrying capacity is affected by the type and size of tourist market (day trippers or destination seekers), the gambling tourist theme being promoted (small, quaint and historic gambling or full-scale entertainment), and location (an urban environment that can more easily absorb potential impacts or a rural community).

♥ **Assess competitiveness.** If gambling is to be more than simply tolerated as an economic development strategy, states must recognize that the gambling industry itself is undergoing fundamental change. Because of the worldwide growth in gambling, the industry is becoming much more competitive. Any decision made to implement limited-stakes (or any) gambling should be based on a realistic assessment of the competitive climate. Competitiveness may be influenced by the presence of or potential for gambling in nearby towns, Indian reservations or neighboring states; as well as by whether that competition will offer higher stakes, a greater variety of games or longer hours. It is also influenced by other forms of gambling that might affect the draw, such as dog and horse racing, off-site sports betting or video lottery terminals. National and local market trends also weigh in—for example, continued interest in gambling, or whether a community offers other attractions that entice visitors who also might gamble.

Who benefits from gambling?

To attract business in a competitive climate, casinos may have to upgrade their appearance, offer quality food and entertainment, provide sleeping rooms or campgrounds, furnish child care or other activities to entertain children, and in general help communities become attractive to potential markets. States and communities must strive to understand what comparative advantages they possess and protect them, determine what the market size is for gambling and not overbuild, identify the most advantageous location(s) for gambling both in terms of capacity and minimizing impacts, and structure a fair but not excessive fee and tax structure.

♥ **Decide who benefits.** "Who benefits from gambling?" is an essential question to answer when crafting state and local strategy concerning gambling. Should the big winners be property owners—some of whom may sell early for large profits and leave? Is historic preservation the primary priority? How can states help local residents benefit from gambling through business ownership and employee development? To what extent should impact funds be distributed to neighboring towns and counties to help handle increased police, fire, housing and social service costs? And how can the financial benefits derived from the gambling industry be equitably distributed throughout the state? To help, states should define as precisely as they can what outcomes are being sought.

States should define as precisely as they can what outcomes are being sought

Once these "What do we want?" questions are answered, planning and implementation can begin in earnest. States must plan for the development and management of the industry, recognizing that the unexpected will likely occur. Lessons that are right today are sure to change tomorrow; the best way to guard against unwelcome outcomes is to put careful effort into deciding what is wanted, designing ways to achieve it, and watching carefully to make mid-course corrections—all the while using the full range of policy tools: zoning and other land use strategies and regulations, grant programs, contracts, awards, technical assistance and reporting requirements.

Hold 'em or Fold 'em

The South Dakota and Colorado experiences, as well as reports from other states with some type of casino-style gambling, make it apparent that gambling *is* "different" from other industries or economic development. It offers the possibility of quick windfalls, for states as well as communities. It raises the red flag of long-standing moral rejection—and the need for policy to deal directly with moral objections so as to avoid ineffective or unanticipated outcomes. And more than most service industries, gambling creates substantial change, both good and bad, in communities.

Perhaps the worst thing a state can do is hope the gambling issue will go away

The stakes involved in implementing gambling are high: substantial public and private investment, a community's well-being and confidence in government. Managing casino gambling is not a game for the faint-hearted. Nor should it be a game of chance. It requires a fair-sized ante, a game plan and skill in playing. The rewards can be great, but so are the risks. And states and communities must be careful not to become addicted to it.

Perhaps the worst thing a state can do is hope the gambling issue will go away, and then, when an initiative passes or a neighboring state's gambling activities put pressure on the homestate legislature, quickly patch together a set of reactions. Instead, states can play a very helpful role by monitoring the health and integrity of the industry, the community's ability to handle issues, the value of the experience to the state's visitors, the effectiveness of service delivery to the communities, and the impacts on the other parts of the state. This guide—less a rulebook and more a lesson on how to keep your eyes open—attempts to help states and communities that are dealing with or considering gambling avoid losing their shirts.

Chapter 1. A Preview of Limited-Stakes Casino Gambling

The Proliferation of Gambling

*Last year [1992], Americans legally bet about $330
billion, up from $178 billion a decade earlier. That
$330 billion surpassed the Defense Department budget
by about $39 billion. And it was $130 billion more
than total sales at grocery stores in 1991.*

Seattle Post-Intelligencer
July 26, 1993

Almost daily, newspapers across the country report
about gambling. Whether it be expansion of Indian
gambling, riverboats, lottery or video lottery terminals,
interest in gambling revenues is driving states to consider
initiating or expanding their gambling opportunities. In
particular, states are realizing the economic potential of
casino-style gambling, and are seeking a portion of the
financial success of the large casino operations in Nevada
and New Jersey (Atlantic City). Recently, eight states
have initiated some type of non-Indian casino gambling,
some of a "limited-stakes" nature—which means that the
maximum bet that can be wagered is capped and the
variety of games offered may be restricted. The states
include Colorado and South Dakota (community-based),
and Iowa, Illinois, Indiana, Louisiana, Mississippi and
Missouri (riverboat gambling).

Today, 48 states allow some form of gambling. In
addition to the ten states with casino gambling, ten states
have approved card rooms; 45 states offer charitable
games including bingo, keno and "Las Vegas nights"; 44
states have horse or dog racing; 21 states have slots or
video slot machines; and 16 states have Class III tribal
gambling that includes casino-style games. New Orleans
recently approved casino gambling, and it appears that
Chicago and Washington, D.C. may not be far behind, as
the mayors of these cities are pushing hard for billion-
dollar entertainment, convention and gambling centers.

Should the proliferation of casino gambling continue at its current pace, every American may soon have access to a casino within a two-hour drive

During the most recent legislative sessions, more than half the states introduced legislation related to gambling. A 1993 nationwide review of proposed legislation affecting gambling, conducted by the National Conference of State Legislatures, found that 24 bills regarding riverboat and offshore gambling have been introduced in 14 states, 75 bills regarding video gambling have been introduced in 28 states, and 36 bills dealing with casino gambling have been introduced in 14 states. Should the proliferation of casino gambling continue at its current pace, every American may soon have access to a casino within a two-hour drive.

Why this Policy Guide?

Because the initial revenues from gambling appear to be so great, many small towns are now looking at gambling as a solution to their economic troubles. In the 1992 Colorado general election alone, there were four ballot initiatives that, had they been approved, would have expanded limited-stakes casino gambling from the current three communities to an additional 27 cities and six counties.

Because policy challenges to states initiating gambling are substantial and the potential economic benefits are great, many are seeking guidance on how to proceed. The gambling industry is volatile. The potential for error is great. And the experience of states and communities in dealing with gambling can still be best described as a mixed bag, poorly understood in economic, social and political terms.

It's not just the volume of gambling activity that makes a state policy guide important; it is the broad-reaching effects that the decision to approve gambling has on a state's people and government capacity.

Although gambling is appearing across the country in a number of forms, two states—South Dakota and Colorado—have implemented limited-stakes casino gambling in small communities, with varying degrees of success. This report looks at the experience of these initial two states, and their respective communities of Deadwood

(South Dakota), and Black Hawk, Central City and Cripple Creek (Colorado). From their experience, it is clear that gambling offers the potential for both significant benefits and costs. And, as would be expected, their decisions have resulted in economic and social tradeoffs, many of which were difficult to anticipate.

This report seeks to provide information to guide states and communities considering gambling, to identify the right questions, and perhaps to provide a few of the answers. It has been prepared because experience with casino gambling across the nation is limited and little has been done to identify and understand what state policy does exist. This report focuses on South Dakota and Colorado because they have developed enough of a track record to be able to illustrate points, draw conclusions and make recommendations to others.

This report seeks to provide information to guide states and communities considering gambling

Design of this Guide

This guide provides specific information about the gambling experience in South Dakota and Colorado and then reflects upon implications for state policy. State policy is discussed in terms of regulations, revenue, economic development, social impacts and planning. This chapter provides an overview of the growth in gambling, the need for guidelines specifically for small towns, and a description of methodology. Chapters 2 and 3 describe the experience of gambling in both the individual towns and their respective states. Chapter 4 presents the findings from the research conducted for this publication. Chapter 5 reflects upon state gambling policies from a general governance perspective, followed by Chapter 6, which discusses state policy strategies for dealing with casino-style gambling. Finally, Chapter 7 lays out the basic options for states to consider as they think about gambling.

Methodology for Assessing Current Policy

The content presented here is based on information secured from a number of sources. Early research conducted in the three Colorado gambling towns documented the perception of local government and agency officials about the social impacts of gambling on the lives of permanent residents.[1] A later study of residents of Gilpin County provided the basis for a comprehensive parks, recreation and tourism master plan, a partial response to the changes brought about by gambling.[2] In addition, numerous visits to each of the communities, coupled with many conversations with residents and public officials and a thorough reading of local newspapers, provided further insight into the issues gambling has raised in these towns.

This project began by convening a workshop attended by experts who represent a variety of viewpoints about gambling, community life and state policy

This specific research project began by convening a workshop attended by experts who represent a variety of viewpoints about limited-stakes gambling, community life and current state policies. These experts reviewed the project design and provided valuable perspectives and clear direction to this overall analysis of state gambling policy. They identified the types of changes that individuals, communities and institutions will potentially experience as a result of gambling. Some changes were of an objective nature, including increases in residential property tax and stress placed on a community's physical infrastructure. Others were of a subjective nature, including the perception of change in residents' political influence and the possibility that youth might develop a "get-rich-quick-and-easy" mentality. This group of experts also identified possible components of a model state policy on gambling.

Second, to update the earlier community research, the residents of Deadwood, Black Hawk, Central City and Cripple Creek were asked to provide their opinions about life in their respective communities since gambling began. Each household was asked to complete a questionnaire consisting of more than 100 questions. This questionnaire sought information about respondents' personal *satisfaction with their community*, including their level of involvement, their sense of safety and security, their degree of affiliation and reward, their attitude about the preservation of local history and their general personal experience with life in a gambling town.

Respondents were also asked to express their *feelings about gambling*, including their level of support for gambling, if and how they benefit, and an assessment of the overall impacts of gambling on their lives and the community. In addition, residents were asked to *assess the changes* that have taken place in their community over the past three years and to what extent they attributed these changes to gambling. This included changes in job opportunities, congestion, cultural exchange, local government services, social life, preservation of history and general changes in the local economy. In addition to demographic information, residents' perceptions were gathered regarding the *type and degree of contact* residents had with gambling and the influence of gambling on their sense of political empowerment.

In order to provide additional perspective on the responses of residents from the gambling towns, similar information was sought from residents of Grand Lake, Colorado, a community that considered but overwhelmingly rejected gambling, yet is also experiencing dramatic change due to the rapid growth of its tourism industry.

Third, local government and casino officials provided their perspectives through participation in focus groups. Recognizing that these two diverse groups have a critical stake in state policy on gambling, casino owners and managers from Black Hawk, Central City and Deadwood, along with local government officials from Black Hawk, Central City, Cripple Creek and Deadwood were asked to provide an in-depth perspective on their needs.

In addition, officials from states that currently offer casino gambling were interviewed via telephone regarding their state policies toward gambling. Their opinions about the administration, regulation, impact assistance and future expansion of gambling, as well as the impact of Indian gaming on state policies, were sought.
Finally, factual information was obtained from state and local agencies that track changes in transportation, law enforcement, social services, safety and employment.

Indian Gaming Regulatory Act

Although this report does not look in detail at the issues states face regarding Indian gambling, the rapid emergence of gambling opportunities on reservations affects a state's policy on gambling.

The Indian Gaming Regulatory Act (IGRA) was enacted in 1988 to provide legal grounds for the establishment of gambling by tribes—the result of more than a decade of intergovernmental battles over the regulation of gambling on reservations. The fundamental argument was one of sovereignty over the regulation of gambling.

The act established three classes of gambling, each with a different regulatory authority based on the relative stakes or interests involved. Class I games are traditional and ceremonial Indian games and are regulated solely by the tribes. Class II games include bingo, lotto, pulltabs and non-bank card games, all of which were already available on many reservations. These are regulated by the National Indian Gaming Commission. Class III games are defined as all other forms of gambling that are not Class I or II, and include lotteries, pari-mutuel betting, slot machines, bank card games, jai alai and other casino games.

Class III games allow the most opportunity for fraud since they involve large cash transactions with the house acting as banker. Any tribe wanting to pursue gambling on their lands must negotiate a compact with the state government first, and states are required to negotiate in "good faith" to reach mutually agreeable conditions. Contested negotiations end up in court or revert to the Secretary of the Interior for decision, depending on the reason for failure.

As this publication goes to print, there is speculation that IGRA will be reconsidered by Congress in 1994. IGRA continues to provide fuel for a heated intergovernmental debate over the management of economic activities on Indian lands. States firmly believe that the regulation of all forms of gambling is a state, not a federal, concern, while tribes continue to resist any form of state control over their sovereignty. Clearly the issue is an extremely delicate one, with no readily agreeable solution on the horizon.

Chapter 2. Gambling on Gambling

The Case Towns

The towns of Deadwood, South Dakota, and Black Hawk, Central City and Cripple Creek, Colorado, all have a rich and colorful mining and gambling history. Each of them experienced the "gold rush," a time in history when the local mining district exploded with wealth, people, services, culture—and stories from which movies are made. This has resulted in their designation by the National Park Service as National Historic Landmarks.

There is a history of excitement, drama and nostalgia in these towns, and a cycle of economic boom and bust. There's the tale of the discovery of gold in 1887 in Cripple Creek by a cowpuncher named Bob Womack, who, while on a drinking spree, sold his claim for $500 and later died penniless. And the story of the famous Saloon #10 in Deadwood where James Butler Hickok, alias "Wild Bill," was shot in the back of the head on August 2, 1876, while playing poker. Stories about the "richest square mile on earth" of Gregory Canyon, located between Black Hawk and Central City. The drama of the great fires of 1874 and 1896 that virtually destroyed Central City and Cripple Creek, respectively.

After pursuing numerous economic revitalization efforts to no avail, these communities turned back to gambling

It was not simply by chance that these towns became the first in the country to initiate limited-stakes casino gambling. It was a matter of reviving a recreation pursuit of the past, with the hope that such action would now "save" their communities. Over several decades, the cities experienced a steady economic decline that included the loss of jobs and local services. They had seen an out-migration of residents in search of a better lifestyle, and the slow decay of buildings with great historical significance. In the late 1980s, after pursuing numerous economic revitalization efforts to no avail, these communities turned back to gambling.

The experience has tested the patience, capacity and ingenuity of residents, government officials, and current and emerging businesses

What have Black Hawk, Central City, Cripple Creek and Deadwood experienced since reviving gambling? The experience has been one of adjustment to change—dramatic change that has tested the patience, capacity and ingenuity of residents, government officials and current and emerging businesses. Their experience has revolved around the need to respond to gambling development that is of a much greater scale than anyone imagined.

The changes that are occurring in the gambling towns parallel in many ways those changes experienced by the energy boomtowns of the 1970s and by some resort communities today—changes of great magnitude within a very short period of time. There have been and will continue to be many social, economic and environmental costs and benefits resulting from these positive and negative changes.

William R. Eadington, professor of economics at the University of Nevada at Reno, observed in the mid-1980s that when gambling comes to town, three things occur: The character and reputation of the host community is undeniably altered because of tourism generated by gambling. Economic activity tends to be concentrated in the geographic vicinity of the gambling district. Individual attitudes toward gambling depend on its improvement or deterioration of personal quality of life.

Experiencing Change: Adjusting to Gambling in South Dakota

Deadwood, with a population of about 1,800, is the county seat of Lawrence County. The town, located in the Black Hills of South Dakota on State Highway 85, about 45 miles from Rapid City, historically has been a central player in the myth of the American West. It was founded as a gold mining camp in 1875, and in addition to Wild Bill Hickok, it became the home of Calamity Jane and Wyatt and Morgan Earp. It is a place that was frequented by many other less notable characters with names like Bummer Dan, Slippery Sam, Jimmy-Behind-the-Deuce, Swede Lena and California Jack.

Deadwood can boast about its telephone system installed in 1879—only one year after the White House had its first telephone installed—and about its early use of electricity, which arrived in 1883. Deadwood's greatest economic boom occurred at the turn of the century, resulting from the development of a cyanide gold extraction process. During that time, landmark hotels and commercial and public buildings were constructed for the 6,000 residents and many visitors.

Progress continued until gold production ceased during World War II, after which Deadwood's population decreased and tourism became the new economy. Fires in the early 1950s destroyed many commercial buildings, the city hall and the famous Deadwood Theater. After being designated a National Historic Landmark in 1961 and being listed on the National Register of Historic Places in 1966, Deadwood further capitalized on its Old West history and its reputation for back-room gambling and prostitution. In 1987, after fires destroyed three important commercial buildings in the heart of the historic district, fire became a symbol of what the future held unless some new economic cure could be found for the ailing town.

Fire became a symbol of what the future held unless some new economic cure could be found for the ailing town

In November 1988, 64 percent of South Dakota's voters approved a constitutional amendment allowing limited-stakes gambling within the city limits of Deadwood. This effort was spearheaded by members of the "Deadwood You Bet" committee, which circulated the petition to place the issue on the ballot. Following statewide voter approval, Deadwood voters had to hold another special referendum to approve the limited card games and slot machines, and had to win at least 60 percent of the votes cast. Gambling began November 1, 1989, with games limited to blackjack, poker and slot machines.

South Dakota gambling legislation limited the number of devices to 30 per building, and limited the maximum single bet to $5.00. It also directed that gambling be incidental to some other business activity. Gambling began with five makeshift establishments. Opening day was covered on all major television networks. Touted by its supporters as a means to supplement the struggling bar business, gambling was an immediate and overwhelming success. Crowds literally stood in line to play the machines.

The requirement that gambling be incidental to other business resulted in many cases in the creation of such "businesses" as restaurants, T-shirt shops, ice cream parlors or some other minimal side business activity in order to comply with the law. Those casinos that attempted to get a license without a secondary business were denied.

Just as no one predicted the overwhelming interest in gambling, the burden that gambling placed on town and county governments was also unexpected

Just as no one predicted the overwhelming interest in gambling, the burden that gambling placed on the town and county governments was also unexpected. Parking, traffic, construction and increased law enforcement activity posed an immediate problem for the city commission, which for a number of years prior to gambling had operated under severe financial constraints.

In addition, the town was faced with efforts to adopt historic preservation and zoning regulations at the same time that dozens of construction and remodeling projects were under way on Main Street. While the gambling legislation allocated a large portion of the fees and taxes from gambling to historic restoration and preservation in Deadwood, the immediate infrastructure needs were greater than the initial funds generated.

To cope with that problem the city issued general revenue bonds, pledging future gambling fees and taxes to repay the bonds. This allowed Deadwood to begin nearly $23 million worth of infrastructure improvements, including three major parking projects, a new city hall, a fire station, a city maintenance shop, a complete restructuring of utilities, sidewalks and brick surfacing of Main Street, and renovation of the municipal recreation center. Within a year, nearly 1,200 new jobs were created within the gambling industry itself and through construction activity.

The gambling boom created other impacts. Crime rates and child-protection calls increased, resulting in the need for more law enforcement, prosecution, court personnel and social services. Property taxes, which some had predicted would decrease, actually increased, in some cases dramatically, due to inflated appraisals caused by the speculative real estate market. The increase in property values drove most existing retail establishments out of existence—or forced them to add gambling devices to their business.

The increased activity in Deadwood, which is geographically constrained due to the surrounding mountainous terrain, caused changes in surrounding communities as well. Retail establishments reopened in other cities and many of the new gambling employees were forced or chose to live outside of Deadwood. Thus, the housing markets in neighboring cities also increased, as did the overall commercial activity in those communities.

The increase in property values drove most existing retail establishments out of existence—or forced them to add gambling devices to their business

Experiencing Change: Adjusting to Gambling in Colorado

Black Hawk and Central City are mountain communities located in Gilpin County about 30 miles west of the Denver metropolitan area. They sit just off State Highway 119, a winding two-lane highway, in a narrow canyon that effectively constrains growth in their downtown central cores and most of their residential areas. The 1990 Census reports a population of 227 for Black Hawk and 335 for Central City. These figures appear to be considerably lower today for Black Hawk, but about the same for Central City. Only a few hotel rooms are available, making this area a day-trip destination. Although these towns share a common border they traditionally have staunchly maintained their separate identities.

Cripple Creek is also a mountain community with a current estimated population of 620 people, up from the 1990 census count of 580. It is located in Teller County about 45 miles west of Colorado Springs on State Highway 67. This stretch of road is narrow and winding as well, and requires travelers to pass through "Little Ike," a one-lane tunnel. The town sits at tree line in a high meadow with open space surrounding it. It is quite isolated, and access in the winter can be unpredictable. There are about 350 hotel rooms in Cripple Creek today, making it both an overnight destination and a day-trip location.

Led by an initial attempt in 1989 by the Central City Preservation, Inc., Committee, these three Colorado cities were unsuccessful in convincing state legislators to amend the Colorado constitution to allow gambling. The committee then secured the required voter signatures statewide to place an initiative on the ballot resulting in the passage of Amendment 4. Approved by 57 percent of the voters in a statewide vote in November 1990, this constitutional amendment allows for limited-stakes poker, blackjack and slot machines.

Gambling has generated tremendous activity in these local economies. At the end of the 1992 fiscal year, there were approximately 12,000 devices in 76 casinos in Colorado, compared to approximately 2,000 devices in 77 casinos in Deadwood. Gambling has raised adjusted gross proceeds (AGP)—that is, the amount of money wagered less the amount paid out in prizes—in 1992 of $155,541,000. Since then, the number of casinos has dropped, reaching a low of 64 with approximately 10,000 devices. During the entire period since gambling began in 1991, 22 casinos have closed. This can be attributed to several factors, including undercapitalization, competition, poor cash flow, mismanagement and acquisition by other gambling properties.

Gambling has generated tremendous economic activity in these local economies. It has also disrupted community life

Gambling disrupted life in these Colorado communities. Construction of and enhancements to infrastructure (water, sewer, streets) and buildings soon to be casinos created tremendous turmoil and inconvenience. Noise, dust and traffic became commonplace. The few existing retail stores, gas stations and traditional social gathering places quickly disappeared. Some long-term residents were displaced when a mobile home park was closed to make room for gambling. In many cases, only the facade of historical structures could be salvaged due to the structural requirements of turning old buildings into high traffic areas. And, due to gambling, the bonded indebtedness of one community—Central City—increased from $580,000 prior to gambling to $23 million today.

In January 1993, a moratorium on building was declared in Central City reputedly due to a shortage of

> "As for the future, I would like to assist the City in focusing on ways to rebuild our community. In my opinion, it is dysfunctional. Central City is divided into two parts: residents and gaming. We need to blend the two and in order to do this, we need something in the middle. We have no parking privilege for the local residents, no grocery stores, gas stations or laundromats. The community cannot go on without services or social activities. If I am elected, I will work towards the goal of having the City turn its energy into finding ways to develop these services."
>
> *City Council Candidate for Central City*
> *Advertisement, October 1993*

water. This action brought about accusations that local politicians, who were also commercial property owners, were making decisions in a manner that was only in their own best financial interests. The result was an unsuccessful recall election. In reality, the moratorium was declared not only because of a limited water supply, but also the need to complete a traffic plan, a growth management plan and a comprehensive plan.

In terms of tourism, government and public officials report that traditional visitors are no longer coming, partially due to the gambling atmosphere and partially because many traditional tourism offerings have disappeared. Even the famous Central City Opera was affected, experiencing an initial decline in attendance, although it appears it now is well on its way to recapturing its lost market. The historic train and autumn aspen tours in Cripple Creek have also fallen victim to a decline in non-gambler visitation.

It was also recently reported that many of Cripple Creek's high school seniors anticipate leaving town after graduation. Young people have been leaving their rural hometowns to pursue the "American Dream" for many years. It was originally hoped that they might remain because of increased job opportunities due to gambling. Because gambling offers few employment opportunities for people under 21, it isn't clear whether gambling jobs can entice youth to stay in their communities.

Because gambling offers few employment opportunities for people under 21, it isn't clear whether gambling jobs can entice youth to stay in their communities

The tourist season, consisting mostly of visitors looking for a gambling experience, is now year-round

Despite some of the negative changes and uncertainties, the economy of these gambling communities is booming. Those over 21 who want a gambling job can have one. The tourist season, consisting mostly of visitors looking for a gambling experience, is now year-round. Buildings—once literally falling down—are being rebuilt. Sales tax revenues have dramatically increased, local events are reappearing again and the state's general fund was $4.1 million richer in 1992.

Certainly there are costs incurred when rapid and dramatic change occurs in a community's development. The belief that gambling would be of a limited nature, coupled with the excitement that economic change would finally be taking place, probably led Colorado residents and decisionmakers to ignore the advice of their predecessors in Deadwood and the energy boomtowns. Doing so meant they did not adequately prepare for the changes they encountered.

Chapter 3. Rules of the Game

This chapter discusses the policies of states other than South Dakota and Colorado with casino-style gambling, and provides an overview of the evolution of state policy and regulatory actions specific to South Dakota and Colorado since approval of gambling, including information about the collection and distribution of revenues, and the stance both states have taken in managing gambling.

The most detailed and factual information available pertains to policies directed toward regulation, enforcement, and revenue collection and distribution. Broader state policies, however, can have an effect on the allocation of funds, the services and technical assistance a state provides, the ease of moving through state procedures, the promotion of gambling activities and residents' perception of gambling in the state.

States have three basic policy stances available. They can be supporters of gambling. They can be policy neutral. Or they can discourage the initiation or expansion of gambling within their boundaries. The decision, if indeed there is a conscious decision that prevails throughout state agencies, results from balancing the desire to reap economic benefits with the concern over moral decline—either real or perceived. Confusion in state policy can result when a conscious, unified or clear decision about gambling is not made.

Confusion in state policy can result when a conscious, unified or clear decision about gambling is not made

Current State Policy on Casino-Style Gambling

State officials from nine of the ten states currently offering one or more forms of limited-stakes community-based casino gambling, riverboat gambling or full-scale casino gambling were surveyed by telephone to determine what state policies were currently in place.[3] (See Figure 1.) The response from these officials revealed interesting variations, and also highlighted the relatively limited role—other than regulation—that states have chosen to play in establishing gambling policy.

As mentioned earlier, three of the states interviewed (Colorado, New Jersey and South Dakota) introduced gambling through a citizens' initiative resulting in a statewide vote. In Illinois, Iowa, Louisiana, Mississippi, Missouri and Nevada, the legislature approved the introduction of gambling.

Virtually all nine states provide a full complement of *regulatory provisions*, including authorization and formation of a state gambling commission, providing license checks, enforcing conduct of allowable games, collecting taxes and performing audits on revenues. In addition, a number of other limits have been set, including building safety standards, size of stakes, number of machines and types of games offered. The regulations are set through a mix of constitutional amendments, statutes and commission requirements.

Figure 1: State Non-Indian Casino Gambling as of October 1, 1993

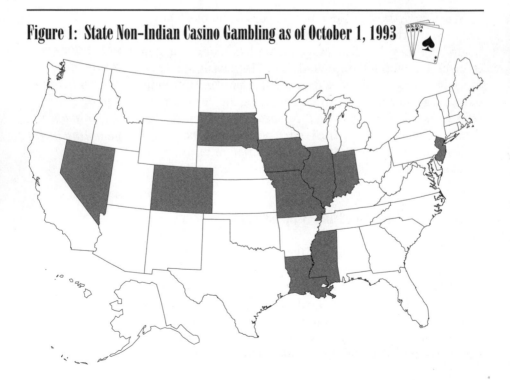

Revenues to states generally are derived from a tax on AGP, device fees, riverboat boarding fees, application and license fees and tap fees for certain services. In turn, once costs for gambling regulation have been covered, states distribute money to state general funds, local communities and counties, and a variety of public purposes—education, historic preservation, seniors and disabled, and assistance for gambling addiction.

Other than revenue sharing from gambling proceeds, states typically provide little in *impact assistance* to communities with gambling. Regular community development block grant funds may be available during start-up and additional monies are almost always provided for law enforcement, but only a few states increase funding for such purposes as highway construction, addiction counseling, job training or other social services. South Dakota did, however, authorize Deadwood to bond against future revenues.

Other than revenue sharing from gambling proceeds, states typically provide little in impact assistance to communities with gambling

The three *most critical issues* state officials identified that states must face were:

♠ the expanding competition emerging in other states and on Indian reservations

♠ the resulting pressures to liberalize regulations

♠ a recognition that gambling itself was maturing into an entertainment industry requiring new strategies to help it adapt and compete.

Other concerns included the potential loss of riverboats to other locations, determining appropriate levels of tax rates and deciding how best to allocate revenues. Nevada personnel expressed a unique concern: how to avoid the pressure of lax gambling industry practices allowed elsewhere from being introduced in Nevada. At present, license holders in Nevada must meet Nevada regulatory standards wherever they do business.

Currently, no state has a *formal mechanism for coordinating* among various state agencies involved with gambling (for example, transportation, economic development, tourism, social services, community development). New Jersey officials reported that their state is creating a commission on gambling policy to oversee such coordination, but it is not yet in place.

Surprisingly, respondents indicated that tribal gambling appears to have little impact on the conduct of non-Indian gambling establishments, nor was it considered to be much of a concern to state gambling commissions. This is despite the fact that almost all these states had or soon will have tribal casinos operating in their jurisdiction. While some states commented on the higher limits allowed on reservations and the inability to tax tribal games, most seemed to think that reservation gambling was either far enough removed or different enough in composition that it wouldn't cause major problems.

This finding seems counterintuitive, given the major political controversies about the functioning of the Indian Gaming Regulatory Act. For instance, in South Dakota, the Commission on Gaming is spending more and more time with the tribal gambling commissions as Indian gambling in that state becomes more pronounced. One full-time employee is currently dedicated to Indian gambling and the commission anticipates that as the law becomes more clearly defined and if states are assigned a larger scope of control over these entities, it will be dedicating even more resources to Indian gambling.

Do your home-work, know what you want, be realistic about the nature of the industry, plan well and then regulate the changes allowed to happen

It may be that the lack of concern expressed about Indian gambling is due to the sample of surveyed states being too small to be representative, that gambling commissions are relatively insulated from having to deal with tribal gambling, or that for states that already have casino gambling, tribal gambling isn't much of an issue.

Finally, when asked about advice for others, the overwhelming advice was *caution*: Do your homework, know what you want, be realistic about the nature of the industry, plan well and then regulate the changes allowed to happen.

Gambling in South Dakota

Policies and Regulations. South Dakota offers a lottery, pari-mutuel racing, statewide video gambling, charitable gambling, limited-stakes casino gambling and tribal gambling on a number of Indian reservations.

As previously mentioned, the ballot initiative that established gambling in Deadwood allows for three kinds of games: blackjack, poker and slot machines. A limit of 30 games and/or machines (devices) is set for each building, and each casino must offer a second business such as gifts, candy, meals or liquor. In addition, strict regulations have been set for approving casino licenses; investigating owners, operators and employees; and enforcing conduct of the operations.

The limit of 30 machines per building led to some unanticipated consequences. Although initiated to keep gambling limited and secondary to other business, Dead-wood was confronted with debates over the definition of a "building." This limit on machines led to the opening of a large number of small casinos.

Deadwood was confronted with debates over the definition of a "building"

In 1990, the South Dakota legislature declared the public policy of the state toward limited–stakes gambling to be:

♣ The success of gaming is dependent upon public confidence and trust that licensed gaming is conducted honestly and competitively, that the rights of the creditors of licenses are protected and that gaming is free from criminal and corruptive elements.

♣ Public confidence and trust can only be maintained by strict regulation of all persons, locations, practices, associations and activities related to the operation of licensed gaming establishments and the manufacture or distribution of gaming devices and equipment.

♣ All establishments where gaming is conducted and where gambling devices are operated, along with manufacturers, sellers and distributors of certain gambling devices and equipment, must therefore be licensed, controlled and assisted to protect the public health, safety, morals, good order and the general welfare of the inhabitants of the state; to foster the stability and success of gaming; and to preserve the economy and policies of free competition of the state of South Dakota.

♣ No applicant for a license or other affirmative commission approval has any right to a license or to the granting of the approval sought. Any license issued or other commission approval granted pursuant to the provisions of this chapter is a revocable privilege, and no holder acquires any vested right therein or thereunder.[4]

Limited-stakes casino gambling in South Dakota is governed by a five-member gaming commission

Limited-stakes casino gambling in South Dakota is governed by a five-member gaming commission which sets state policy and oversees gambling activities in Deadwood and for pari-mutuel racing, and has limited authority over Indian gambling. This gaming commission sets and enforces the rules for casino gambling, processes and approves applications, and provides for revenue collection and audit.

Under the direction of the Executive Secretary, the Commission on Gaming employs 15 full-time employees who regulate casino gambling: five who are sworn law enforcement agents, four auditors and the rest, support staff. There also are several part-time employees who work the racetracks. The costs associated with regulating these forms of gambling are covered by the revenues from gambling in Deadwood.

Currently, five of the nine South Dakota Indian reservations have casinos. As a result of the negotiated compacts, the gaming commission is responsible for conducting background investigation on all individuals involved in the licensing process, inspecting all devices to ensure they meet state specifications, conducting a certain number of hours of on-site inspections and investigations, assisting tribes with any endeavor related to gambling when they request assistance and enforcing the provisions of the compact.

Promulgation of Rules (South Dakota)

   The gaming commission may promulgate rules for the orderly transaction and conduct of its business and the substantive rules that it may determine proper concerning the issuance, revocation and suspension of gaming licensees; the division of machines or card games that may be placed in any building or retail business; the conduct and operation of limited card games and slot machines; and any other things necessary to carry out the purposes of this chapter.

   The commission may also promulgate rules necessary to administer complaints that may be received from the public and conduct such other investigations and inspections into the conduct of the games and the licensees and the maintenance of the equipment as the commission may deem necessary and proper. The commission's rules may provide procedures for summary suspension of any license issued under this chapter and shall provide for subsequent contested case hearings before suspensions become final or a license is revoked. The commission may apply for injunctive or declaratory relief to enforce the provisions of this chapter and any rules promulgated thereunder. Action by the commission may not limit the authority of the state's attorney or attorney general from enforcing criminal actions.

   Video lottery, scratch tickets and Lotto America (Power Ball) are regulated by a separate Lottery Commission. South Dakota also authorizes charitable gambling through minimal statutory provisions. Currently there are no regulatory standards for charitable gambling and the monitoring of this activity is basically ignored by the state. Although efforts have been made by a few legislators to regulate this form of gambling, they have all been defeated in the legislature.

Revenues. South Dakota levies an eight-percent tax on the adjusted gross revenues (AGR—a different term for what Colorado calls adjusted gross proceeds) of Deadwood's casinos. This tax is determined by the Commission on Gaming but cannot be lower than five percent or higher than 15 percent. Initially set by the legislature, the eight-percent gaming tax would only be changed if current conditions change, for example, if the administrative needs of the commission increase or if Deadwood should need more financial resources for preservation.

Of the eight-percent gross revenue tax, 40 percent goes directly to the general fund of South Dakota and 10 percent to Lawrence County. The balance of this tax plus all other revenues—including a $2,000 annual device fee—go into a Commission on Gaming Fund. After administrative expenses are deducted, the remainder goes to Deadwood for historic restoration and preservation, which by statute is to be "interpreted liberally in scope and effect."

Although the purpose for which Deadwood can expend its share of state gambling revenues is strictly controlled by statute, the county and state can expend their shares in whatever manner they choose

All of Deadwood's expenditures must be approved by the state through its Historical Preservation Center based on the rules adopted by the State Historical Society. Although the purpose for which Deadwood can expend its share of state gambling revenues is strictly controlled by statute, the county and state can expend their shares in whatever manner they choose.

In 1992, after administrative costs of $861,700, Deadwood received more than $5 million in the final distribution of AGR and other related gambling revenues. The State of South Dakota General Fund received $1.2 million, and Lawrence County almost $300,000. Thus the city of Deadwood received 68 percent of the money, the state 16 percent, the county 4 percent. Administrative costs totaled 12 percent. (See Figure 2.) This is in contrast to FY 1989 (eight months of activity) when Deadwood received $1.85 million, the state general fund $446,800, and the county $111,700, with administrative and start-up costs for the Commission on Gaming totaling $509,700.

State's Stance. Looking beyond policies, regulation and revenues, South Dakota appears to have had a generally neutral stance toward gambling. Initially, state officials were concerned with the potential for organized crime and other negative impacts. As a result, they gave little in terms of assistance or breaks to gambling. At the same time, they did not want to make it difficult for gambling to succeed, so fees were set at what was presumed to be a reasonable level. Deadwood was also allowed to bond on anticipated

Figure 2: South Dakota Commission on Gaming, Distribution of Revenues FY 92

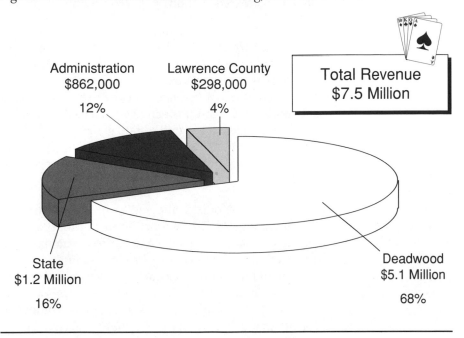

Administration
$862,000
12%

Lawrence County
$298,000
4%

Total Revenue
$7.5 Million

State
$1.2 Million
16%

Deadwood
$5.1 Million
68%

revenues, making it possible to begin providing necessary infrastructure before actual revenues were distributed.

The state's neutral stance has allowed Deadwood to exercise its own leadership and direction. Casino operators and employees have been encouraged to become active in city government. In addition, the gambling industry has developed a number of its own committees. There seems to be recognition by the gambling industry of the value of helping the town stabilize and in diversifying activities and services that will attract a variety of tourist markets.

Deadwood has created the type of gambling industry it said it would. As gambling's record as a clean industry grows, and people become more familiar with gambling and its economic value to the state, it is reasonable to expect that the state will develop more supportive policies. Indeed, that was the case recently when the South Dakota Legislature approved changes to increase gambling. Although the voters reversed this effort in a statewide vote, the legislature's passage of the bill reflects lawmakers' increased support.

The May 1993 bill would have expanded gambling in Deadwood and affected the distribution of future revenues. The bill raised the limits on games, set a $5.6 million baseline for Deadwood, then allowed for a sliding scale split of additional revenues between Deadwood and the state until a 50/50 ratio is achieved. The additional revenues would have gone to the state general fund with the intention of using them to support tourism, although the bill did not specifically dedicate the revenue for that purpose.

The bill also would have allowed an increase in the number of gaming devices and bet limits at tribal casinos and expanded space and machine limits to accommodate what is referred to as the Dunbar Project—a large-scale complex including a resort, casino and convention center to be located on the edge of Deadwood. (See *The Dunbar Project*.) In actuality, this legislation would have allowed any facility that met statutory guidelines to take advantage of the provisions. The legislation was placed on a September 1993 ballot via a citizens' initiative, but was defeated by a 58–42 percent margin. There was an east river/west river (Missouri River) voter split with the more populated eastern section voting against expansion.

There appears to be an emerging anti-gambling sentiment in South Dakota that was first evident in the attempt to repeal the use of video lottery terminals in 1992

Several possible reasons may explain why this initiative failed. First, there appears to be an emerging anti-gambling sentiment in South Dakota, first evident in the attempt to repeal the use of video lottery terminals in 1992. Low voter turnout for the 1993 initiative strengthened the impact of the anti-expansion coalition vote. Second, some may oppose increasing gambling limits on the Indian reservations, which the initiative would have allowed. Third, the initiative was pushed heavily by the pro-gambling element, whose aggressive stance may have alienated some voters. Finally, with the substantial financial resources dedicated solely to historic restoration and preservation in Deadwood, residents of other communities may be jealous of Deadwood's financial windfall. (See Figure 3.)

The Dunbar Project

The Dunbar Project, also referred to as the "Costner Project" after principals Dan and Kevin Costner, was a proposed $65 million tourism destination resort for Deadwood, South Dakota. Financing would have come directly from the Costners and included no other major equity backers. Slated for opening in May 1996, this resort, convention center and casino complex was to be built within the city limits on 85 acres of land. Sixty acres were to be left in a somewhat natural state that would have included hiking trails and other outdoor activities. This upscale resort was intended to fill an untapped market niche providing a pleasure and business travel destination that goes beyond the current "rubber-tire" market of the Black Hills region.

This proposed development would have totaled 411,000 square feet of which 11,000 was slated for gambling. The gambling area was designed to hold approximately 300 devices, the maximum number allowable by the state under the proposed qualified convention center license. The complex would have added an additional 320 sleeping rooms to the roughly 400 currently available in Deadwood. It also included restaurants, child care facilities, bowling alley, outdoor live theater, cinemas and an 18-hole golf course. Through leasing arrangements with existing railways, the Dunbar Project would have included a tourist railroad from Rapid City to the complex and on into Deadwood. About 70 percent of this rail system is in place, with approximately nine miles of new rail construction needed along leased railroad right of ways. Water and sewer were to be financed by the town.

Undoubtedly, a resort project of this nature would have far-reaching economic benefits for the already popular Black Hills region. The Costners estimated this project would have created an additional 600-650 new full-time jobs, generating approximately $12 million in payroll annually, with multiplying effects in the range of $250 million. They projected a marketing budget larger than that of the state itself. The Dunbar Project was effectively defeated when South Dakota citizens rejected a gambling expansion bill in 1993.

Figure 3: South Dakota Gaming Tax Revenues and Distribution, FY 1990–1992

	FY 1990	FY 1991	FY 1992
TOTAL GAMING REVENUES	$14,330,125	$33,070,870	$38,619,946
DISTRIBUTION			
Lawrence County (10% of 8% on AGR)	$70,768	$227,110	$298,335
State General Fund (40% of 8% on AGR)	$223,696	$967,814	$1,193,419
City of Deadwood	$1,850,000	$5,047,328	$5,123,279
NUMBER OF CASINOS	45	83	77

The stability of the gambling industry in Deadwood is still unknown. With changes sure to come, state policy likely will continue to evolve.

Gambling in Colorado

Policies and Regulations. Colorado law currently allows a state lottery, pari-mutuel racing, and limited stakes casino gambling in three rural towns. In addition, compacts have been negotiated by the Ute Mountain Utes and the Southern Utes with the governor to allow casino gambling on their respective reservations. Charitable gambling, other than charity nights operated by casinos, was closed down some years ago and pulltabs, bingo and raffles are regulated by the Secretary of State.

Limited-stakes gambling in Colorado is regulated by the Division of Gaming, a division of the Colorado Department of Revenue, and is subject to the administrative and operating rules that govern all state agencies. The division is responsible for the regulation and enforcement of limited stakes gambling and maintains a staff of 54, with offices in Denver, Cripple Creek and Central City/ Black Hawk. Thirty-four of the division's employees are responsible for investigations, background checks and monitoring for organized crime.

The Division of Gaming conducts the investigation of gambling license applicants and is involved with day-to-day activities of limited-stakes gambling. It also oversees the charitable gambling activities of casinos; licensed establishments can sponsor up to 30 charitable events in any one year.

The Colorado Limited Gaming Control Commission is a five-member commission appointed by the governor. The commission oversees the operation of the Division of Gaming and is responsible for promulgating the rules and regulations that govern limited-stakes gambling in the state. Regulations include strict requirements for applications, licensing, oversight and enforcement as well as interpreting building safety standards and the amount of space devoted to gambling. In addition, the commission oversees the compacts negotiated by the two Indian tribes in Colorado with the governor, which includes conducting background investigations on all non-tribal personnel. It also has the authority to continually audit and monitor Indian gambling operations.

According to the Limited Gaming Act, the commission must include an attorney with experience in regulatory law, a certified public accountant with knowledge of corporate finance, a law enforcement official, a corporate manager with five years of business experience and a registered voter.

The gaming commission must interpret the 35–50 percent space allocation for devices—which determines the scale of the gambling industry

The gaming commission must interpret the 35–50 percent space allocation requirement for devices—which, in effect, determines the scale of the gambling industry. This space allocation rule states that no more than 50 percent of any single floor and 35 percent of the total square footage of any building may be devoted to gambling. Also under the commission's authority is the determination of the gaming tax, which, by statute, cannot exceed 40 percent of AGP. In setting the tax rate the commission is required to consider:

♦ the need to provide monies to the cities of Black Hawk, Central City and Cripple Creek for historic restoration and preservation

♦ the impact of gambling on the communities and any state agency including, but not limited to, infrastructure, law enforcement, environment, public health and safety, education, human services and other components due to limited gaming

♦ the impact on licensees and the profitability of their operations

♦ the profitability of the other "for profit" forms of gambling in the state

♦ the profitability of similar forms of gambling in other states

♦ the expenses of the commission and the division for their administration and operation.

All ongoing expenses for the Division of Gaming and the gaming commission are to be paid from monies in the Limited Gaming Fund before any other allocations are made

Revenues. In the first year (October 1991 through September 1992), Colorado implemented a three-tier graduated tax structure which taxed the first $440,000 in AGP at four percent, the amount between that and $1.2 million at eight percent, and any amount over $1.2 million at 15 percent. In the second year, a two-tier structure was put in place to tax AGP under $1 million at two percent and anything more than $1 million at 20 percent.

Beginning in October 1993, the state gaming commission added middle tiers for the mid-size casinos and reduced the top rate as well. The tax rate was adjusted, taxing those casinos earning up to $1 million at two percent (eight casinos), those earning up to $2 million at eight percent (20 casinos), those earning up to $3 million at 15 percent (14 casinos), and those earning more than $3 million at 18 percent (28 casinos). (See Figure 4.)

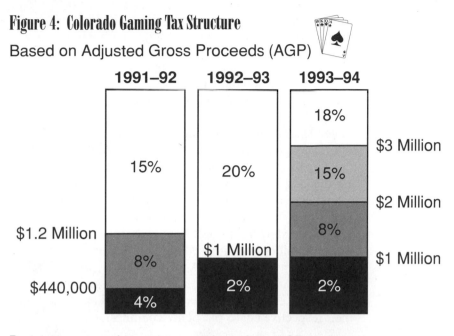

Figure 4: Colorado Gaming Tax Structure

Based on Adjusted Gross Proceeds (AGP)

| 1991–92 | 1992–93 | 1993–94 |

1991–92: 15%, $1.2 Million, 8%, $440,000, 4%

1992–93: 20%, $1 Million, 2%

1993–94: 18%, $3 Million, 15%, $2 Million, 8%, $1 Million, 2%

Percentages equal tax rate on each casino's AGP

The state collects a device fee, application and annual license fees, and other charges. The initial state device fee per slot machine, blackjack and poker table was $100; this was raised in FY 1992 to $150 and lowered again to $100 for FY 1993. All ongoing expenses for the Division of Gaming and the gaming commission are to be paid from monies in the Limited Gaming Fund—the fund set up to hold the state's gaming tax revenue—before any other allocations are made. In addition, prior to the distribution of revenues annually from the Limited Gaming Fund, an amount equal to all expenses of the administration for the preceding two-month time period shall be retained to ensure adequate funding of the commission's activities.

By law, the Limited Gaming Fund is distributed to the State General Fund (49.8 percent), to the Colorado Tourism Promotion Fund (0.2 percent), to the State Historical Fund (28 percent), to the counties in proportion to the gaming revenues generated (12 percent), and to Black

Hawk, Central City and Cripple Creek (10 percent), also in proportion to the revenues generated. (See Figure 5.)

Due to the projected impacts upon counties adjacent to those within which the gambling towns are located, a Contiguous County Limited Gaming Impact Fund was created. In FY 1992, this impact fund received 9.6 percent of the State General Fund gambling revenues or about $425,000. In FY 1993 this amount increased to $1.8 million. Half of this impact fund allocation goes proportionately to the eight contiguous counties based upon the number of casino employees residing in each county. The remaining monies are distributed on a competitive basis with proposals evaluated by the Impact Fund Advisory Committee. This committee is composed of the Executive Directors of the Departments of Local Affairs, Social Services, Highways and Public Safety, in addition to one resident from each of the eight contiguous counties, each appointed by their respective board of county commissioners.

Figure 5: Colorado Gaming Tax Revenue Distribution

Percentage of Gambling Revenues

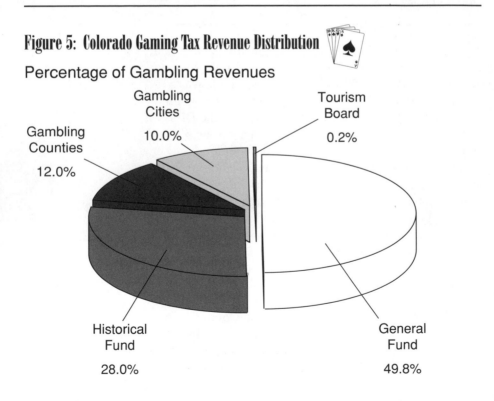

Gambling Cities 10.0%

Tourism Board 0.2%

Gambling Counties 12.0%

Historical Fund 28.0%

General Fund 49.8%

In May 1993, Montezuma and LaPlata Counties were added as contiguous counties due to the expansion of gambling to the Ute Mountain Ute Indian reservation. Although these counties do not participate in the prescribed formula for revenue distribution, they can apply for grants based upon need. It is anticipated that Archuleta County, which is contiguous to the Southern Ute reservation on which a casino was recently opened, will also be added to the contiguous county organization.

The Colorado Historical Society administers the Colorado State Historical Fund, a new state-funded grants program established with the passage of gambling. This fund is intended to foster heritage preservation through tangible and highly visible projects for direct and demonstrable public benefit. The society makes grants primarily to public entities, except that the society may make grants to persons in the private sector so long as the person requesting the grant makes application through a municipality or a county. Twenty percent of this fund is distributed to the communities of Black Hawk, Central City and Cripple Creek for local historic preservation projects, with the remaining 80 percent distributed on a competitive basis across the state. In FY 1992, over $500,000 was returned to the three gambling towns for historic preservation, while $2.4 million was distributed throughout Colorado.

In FY 1993, Colorado's limited gaming revenue grew to $35.5 million

In summary, in FY 1992, Colorado's limited gaming revenue—that is, state tax revenue derived from the percentage tax on adjusted gross proceeds along with license fees, state device fees and fines—totaled almost $13.5 million. After administrative costs of $3.4 million, two months' escrow of $875,000 and a fund deficit of $68,500 were deducted, $9.1 million was available for distribution. The state General Fund received $4.1 million, state Historical Society $2.5 million, Gilpin and Teller Counties $1.1 million, Black Hawk, Central City and Cripple Creek $910,000, the Colorado Tourism Promotion Fund $18,000, and the Contiguous County Impact Fund $425,000.

In FY 1993, the limited gaming revenue grew to $35.5 million. Administrative costs were $5 million, and the two months' escrow for operating expenses totaled $907,000. The State General Fund received $13.4 million, State Historical Society $8.5 million, Gilpin and Teller Counties $3.6 million, Black Hawk, Central City and Cripple Creek $2.9 million, the Colorado Tourism Promotion Fund $61,000, and the Contiguous County Impact Fund $1.7 million. (See Figure 6.)

State's Stance. State policy in Colorado has been perceived in a number of circles as being non-supportive of gambling, in fact, even hostile in nature. For example, total taxes on gambling are the highest in the nation, liquor licensing has very restrictive provisions, and state-supported technical assistance is seen as going to the contiguous counties but not those with gambling. Hours of operation are restricted by statute to between 8:00 a.m. and 2:00 a.m.

Figure 6: Colorado Gaming Tax Revenues and Distribution, FY 1992–93

	FY 1992*	FY 1993
Total Gaming Revenues (taxes, license fees, application fees, background investigation, fines, other)	$13,458,606	$35,546,314
Distribution		
State General Fund	4,114,136	13,424,676
Escrow (Two Months)	875,225	907,622
Administration of Gaming Activities	3,400,093	5,034,531
State Historical Fund (20% of which is returned to gambling cities)	2,552,124	8,534,228
State Tourism Board	18,229	60,959
Contiguous County Fund	425,000	1,754,059
Gilpin County	790,095	2,648,049
Teller County	303,673	1,009,477
Black Hawk	263,783	1,138,405
Central City	394,629	1,067,998
Cripple Creek	253,061	842,536

*Figures represent nine months of gambling activity.

A three-year rolling average of court case demand, which determines funding, means that courts did not have resources available to them during their transition with gambling to deal with the onslaught of cases involving property transactions, fraud and other crimes. Taxation based on highest-and-best-use rather than on actual use drove all retail establishments from Central City and Black Hawk, and most from Cripple Creek.

Taxation based on highest-and-best use rather than on actual use drove all retail establish-ments from Central City and Black Hawk, and most from Cripple Creek

The state distributed no revenues to either the towns or counties until almost a year after the start of gambling, despite the need for financial resources for comprehensive planning, new water and sewer systems, parking areas, construction of roads and other major improvements.

The changes each year by the state in both the level of AGP tax and device fees has created uncertainty within the industry, a factor recognized by the commission in its decision to adjust rates downward for the third year. Despite providing 5,200 new jobs in the services and attractions industry, gambling has no representation on the state tourism advisory board. And, in one of the more unique restrictions, no one associated with gambling is allowed to hold local public elected office. Gambling industry representatives feel that recent reports from the Department of Revenue on casino profits have failed to factor out the 22 casino failures, and that the department is inflating profitability.

While these policies have been interpreted as restrictive and presenting multiple barriers, Colorado has tried to be helpful with a number of other steps. Prior to implementing gambling, teams of decisionmakers were sent to Deadwood to learn from its experience. Initially, Colorado put together a coordination effort involving various state agencies, but reported mixed need and success. Also, Colorado is the only state with a program to provide assistance to contiguous counties.

The state did send technical assistance teams to the communities starting gambling, but members report they were not widely welcomed. Initially, funds were made available through community development block grants and other state programs available to all communities. Additional funding did go to the state highway department and state patrol. The provision that gambling revenues be used to help mitigate the impacts on contiguous counties as well as the policy of distributing funds for historic preservation efforts throughout the state has helped to spread the wealth and good will.

Other provisions, which may have been well-intentioned, seem to be suffering from the law of unintended consequences. Regulatory requirements applied to the gambling industry appear to have driven out the smaller, often locally owned, operations (referred to as mom and pop establishments), forced others to bring in outside investors, or forced expansion in an attempt to earn sufficient revenues to cover costs.

A decision by the gaming commission to allow casinos to calculate maximum square footage devoted to gambling on the basis of machines and game space—and not include aisles, counting rooms, cashier cages and other associated spaces—meant that owners could fit many more machines on the floor. Combined local and state device fees also seem to have benefited the more profitable operations since smaller operators have had to remove machines because they can't cover the fees.

One of the most problematic regulations passed by the legislature prevents anyone associated with gambling from holding local public office

"A problem of a more serious nature is Black Hawk's declining population. According to city clerk Penny Round, 'We need more citizens to at least guarantee a pool to draw from for council and commission positions.'"
Gilpin Weekly Register Call, Gilpin County, Colorado

As mentioned earlier, one of the most problematic regulations passed by the legislature prevents anyone associated with gambling from holding local public office. The rationale for this regulation was to prevent the industry from "taking over" these small towns or from unduly benefiting from local political decisions. However, because of the small population of these communities (Black Hawk is estimated to now have less than 100 residents), there remains only a very small pool of residents from which to draw for political office. The result can be "burned out" residents who are asked to serve repeatedly, the over-representation of minority viewpoints because they are the only ones able or willing to serve, uninformed decisionmaking based upon inadequate information and lack of understanding of the industry, and the disenfranchisement of industry employees.

> "I didn't think we should use gaming as a form of taxing people. I didn't think gaming could be contained in the three areas and I thought it was environmentally bad."
>
> *Colorado Governor Roy Romer*

It may be that many of the problems in Colorado are a result of Colorado-specific factors: the widely reported opposition of the governor which was perceived as equivalent to state policy, the historic parochial disputes between Black Hawk and Central City which seem to have carried over to gambling, and the severe geographic and demographic limits on all three of the towns. At the same time, the outcomes suggest that other states considering gambling be careful about what they put in place, be attentive to the initial results, and be responsive and adaptive as they progress.

It should be noted that positive results have come from some of the problems Colorado has faced. Casino owners have organized to address the issues facing their industry and are presenting a better case for gambling. They are providing more outreach activities and amenities to the communities, taking a more active role in regional and state tourism efforts and generally working together for the good of their cause.

All three gambling towns seem to recognize that they have much to gain by cooperating

Although Black Hawk and Central City continue to disagree and compete on certain issues, all three gambling towns seem to recognize that they have much to gain by cooperating. Black Hawk and Central City have joined with Gilpin County to address the parks, recreation and tourism development issues through a memorandum of understanding, and public officials now hold regular joint meetings. Local governments have grown in their sophistication and ability to manage their towns. Finally, the State Gaming Commission appears to be making more of an effort to learn about the industry, the towns and what are reasonable industry regulations and taxes.

Figure 7: Gambling in South Dakota and Colorado—Pertinent Facts

Fact	South Dakota	Colorado
Citizen Initiative	Yes	Yes
Statewide Vote	Yes	Yes
Date of Vote	November 1988	November 1990
Community Vote	Yes	No
Gambling Begins	November 1989	October 1991
Indian Gambling	Yes – 5 reservations	Yes – 2 reservations
State Commission	Yes – 5 members appointed by governor	Yes – 5 members appointed by governor
Number of Devices	30 Per Establishment	Determined by pct. of building space (35/50%)
Device Fee – *State*	$2,000	$100
Device Fee – *Local*	No	Varies by community
Number of Devices – 1992	1,925	12,000
Number of Casinos – 1992	77	76
State Tax Level	8%	Based on casino revenues; has changed annually: FY91/92 – 4, 8, & 15% FY92/93 – 2 & 20% FY93/94 – 2, 8, 15 & 18%
Revenue Distribution	State General Fund Lawrence County Deadwood Historic Preservation	State General Fund Gilpin & Teller Counties Black Hawk, Central City & Cripple Creek State Tourism Promotion State Historic Preservation
1990 Population of Community	Deadwood 1,800	Black Hawk 227 Central City 335 Cripple Creek 580

Chapter 4. Ante Up: Perspective from the Players

Introducing any new industry into a community can have an immediate and dramatic effect on the lives of permanent residents. Introducing limited-stakes casino gambling in a small rural community, especially if it is large-scale and high-volume, creates significant economic and social change. Its impact on the community can be profound. Many residents of Deadwood and the Colorado gambling towns had become accustomed to a slow-paced, seldom-interrupted, close-knit community style of living. While this lifestyle was comfortable, it unfortunately provided little hope for an improved economy.

Introducing limited-stakes casino gambling in a small rural community, especially if it is large-scale and high-volume, creates significant economic and social change

Gambling was initiated in both South Dakota and Colorado to improve economic conditions for local residents of the communities where it was approved, as well as to restore and preserve historical structures. Although not addressed specifically in the legislation, these initiatives were intended to improve the quality of life generally in these communities.

But the final assessment of the quality of community life goes well beyond just residents' satisfaction with the local economy. In an effort to more clearly understand how introducing gambling into a community affects the perceptions and attitudes of residents about community

The Cause for Legalization: Best Intentions

The intention of the original gambling legislation in South Dakota and Colorado was that legalized gambling would:

♥ diversify the economic and visitor attraction base of the communities

♥ provide funding for restoration/preservation of historic buildings

♥ bring economic success to the depressed communities

♥ provide tax revenue for the state

life, the authors conducted a resident survey in each of the four gambling towns. A head of household member was asked to respond to a series of questions about changes that had taken place in the community over the past three years and to what extent these changes could be attributed to gambling.[5]

In order to provide a context and additional perspective to the information collected from the gambling communities, residents from a non-gambling community were surveyed. Grand Lake, Colorado, was selected because it also has been experiencing the effects of rapid and dramatic change accompanying the growth of its local tourism industry. Grand Lake provided a good comparison because it is similar in population, geography and dependence on a tourism economy—and because it was one of 27 towns and six counties appearing on the statewide 1992 ballot to consider expansion of gambling. Grand Lake differed, however, in that 70 percent of its local voters had rejected gambling in the non-binding referendum.

This chapter summarizes findings from the household survey conducted with residents of the case towns and the non-gambling comparison community

This chapter summarizes findings from the household survey conducted with residents of the case towns and the non-gambling comparison community, combined with factual information collected from county and state data bases.[6] It also presents the findings from focus groups conducted separately with casino and local government officials from the gambling communities.

The Resident Survey: Methodology

The community research effort was designed to determine the perceptions and attitudes of the residents of the four gambling communities regarding the impacts of limited-stakes casino gambling on community life. The questionnaires themselves were based upon information extracted from an extensive literature review of impacts research (primary focus on tourism impacts) and upon questionnaires utilized in prior research by both the authors and other respected researchers. A panel of experts reviewed the survey instrument and the researchers pilot-tested it prior to using it in the communities.

The survey questionnaire was designed to capture the major concerns identified in previous rural community energy and tourism impact research. This prior research sought the perceptions and attitudes of residents who had experienced rapid and dramatic change due to the introduction of a new industry. In the case of this gambling research effort, residents of the four gambling communities were asked to express their feelings about the changes they had experienced since gambling was approved. Grand Lake residents were asked to project the impact that introducing gambling would have on life in their community.

Residents of the four gambling communities were asked to express their feelings about the changes they had experienced since gambling was approved

A team of trained data collectors hand-delivered the questionnaire to residents in Black Hawk, Central City, Grand Lake and Deadwood, and arranged a convenient pick-up time with the head of household. Up to three attempts at different times on different days were made in order to make the initial personal contact. If no contact was made, a questionnaire, a self-addressed stamped envelope and an explanation letter were left at the household. If no reply was received, the team asked local officials to verify occupancy, and attempted personal contact one additional time. In Cripple Creek, the questionnaire was mailed to households. Due to the initial response (70 percent), no follow-up mailing was necessary.

The data collectors attempted to alternate male/female head of household responses where possible. They were also instructed to administer an abbreviated six-question version of the survey instrument, if possible, should the head of household refuse or be unable to complete the full questionnaire. Detailed code sheets were kept to determine the status of the process in each community. Once all questionnaires were collected, a commercial data entry company entered and verified the data. It was then "cleaned" and analyzed using the Statistical Package for the Social Sciences (SPSS).

Residents' interest in the survey was particularly high, as exemplified by the response rate. The usable surveys returned represented high percentages of total occupied households: Black Hawk, 57 percent; Central City, 60 percent; Cripple Creek, 70 percent; Deadwood, 74 percent;

and Grand Lake, 66 percent.[7] In addition to this response, a number of households elected to complete an abbreviated six-question version of the full questionnaire, most likely choosing the abbreviated form because of time limitations, a desire not to fill out a full questionnaire or the inability to do so.[8] These responses to the shortened version provided assurance that these residents' perceptions and attitudes were very similar to those of residents who completed the longer version.

Residents of the four gambling communities did not indicate a strong anti-gambling sentiment

Residents' General Feelings about Gambling

The residents of the four gambling communities did not indicate a strong anti-gambling sentiment.[9] When asked whether their town had made the right choice to develop gambling, whether their town would have had a future without gambling, whether gambling had made their town a better place to live and whether gambling was a pleasure to have in their town, Deadwood residents, on average, were neutral, while Colorado residents were less positive. (See Figure 8.) Grand Lake residents were much more negative about gambling.

Figure 8: Community Support for Gambling

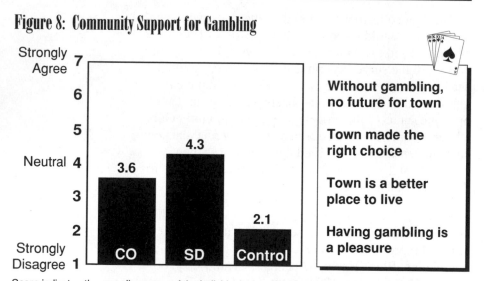

Score indicates the overall average of the individual average response to the four referenced questions.

In addition, residents of both Deadwood and the Colorado towns disagreed strongly with the statements that gambling was inappropriate for their community, that it was hard for them to accept gambling, and that they were embarrassed they lived in a gambling community. (See Figure 9.) When one considers that these communities have historically had gambling and that in the case of Deadwood over 70 percent of the residents voted in favor of gambling in the local referendum, this sentiment is not surprising.

Figure 9: Resident Feelings about Gambling

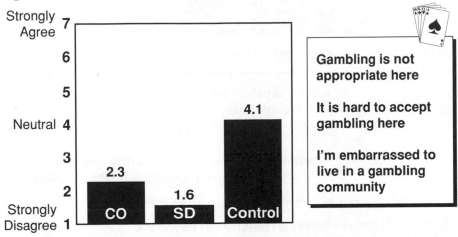

Score indicates the overall average of the individual average response to the three referenced questions.

But residents from the two states showed less approval when asked if they were receiving economic, social or overall personal benefits from gambling. (See Figure 10.) Colorado residents felt that traditional tourists no longer came to their town, that many people had moved away because of gambling and that most of the money from gambling goes to outsiders.

Crowding and Congestion. Residents of all the communities identified the level of crowding and congestion as an area of notable change and concern.

In Deadwood and the Colorado towns alike, citizens indicated they had experienced a large increase in the size

Figure 10: Personal Benefits from Gambling

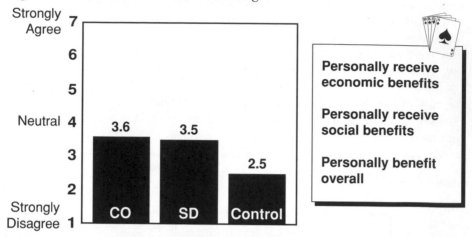

Score indicates the overall average of the individual average response to the three referenced questions.

Personally receive economic benefits

Personally receive social benefits

Personally benefit overall

of crowds in public areas, in noise levels, in the number of driving hazards in the area, and in the level of traffic congestion since gambling. (See Figure 11.)

When asked specifically about traffic congestion, more than 90 percent of the respondents from the gambling

Figure 11: Perceived Changes in Crowding and Congestion

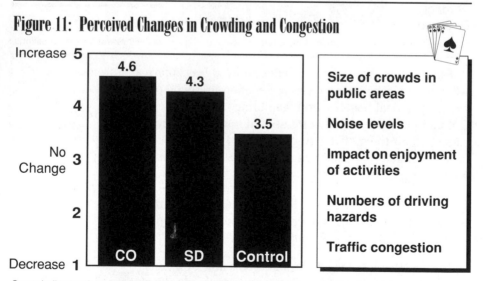

Score indicates the overall average of the individual average response to the five referenced questions.

Size of crowds in public areas

Noise levels

Impact on enjoyment of activities

Numbers of driving hazards

Traffic congestion

communities answered that traffic congestion had increased substantially and that this change was attributable
to gambling. (See Figure 12.)

These perceptions are well supported by traffic count
data collected by the Colorado Department of Transportation. On State Highway 119 going to Central City and
Black Hawk from the Denver metropolitan area, the
average daily traffic for the month of October increased
from just over 3,000 vehicles per day in 1990 (prior to
gambling) to nearly 9,000 vehicles per day in 1991. This
represents almost a 200-percent increase in traffic during
gambling's first month.

In June 1992, nine months into gambling in Colorado,
this average daily vehicle count peaked at just over
12,500. Cripple Creek had similar increases in traffic on
State Highway 67. In June 1991, three months before
gambling began, there was an average of just over 2,000
vehicles per day. Just one year later that figure rose to
nearly 7,000 vehicles per day on this narrow mountain road.

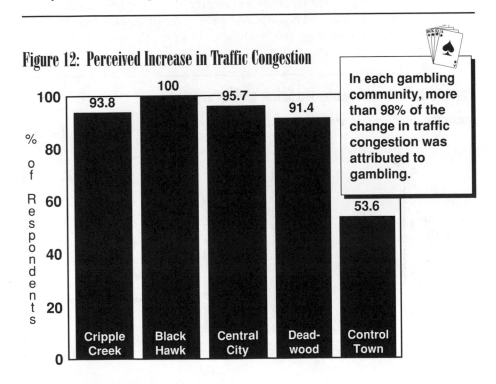

Figure 12: Perceived Increase in Traffic Congestion

In each gambling community, more than 98% of the change in traffic congestion was attributed to gambling.

A permanent traffic counter placed by the South Dakota Department of Transportation at the east end of Main Street in Deadwood showed substantial increases in traffic levels. In 1988, the year before gambling began, the average daily traffic was 6,910 vehicles. That number nearly doubled by 1992, which saw an average of 12,880 vehicles per day; 1991 was the peak year, registering just over 13,000 vehicles daily.

Dust, noise and local traffic congestion were of a scale never imagined or previously experienced by local residents

This increase in traffic inevitably leads to increases in the size of crowds, traffic hazards, noise and parking problems. As one person interviewed said, "Parking is a problem—Americans like to see their cars!" In addition, the massive construction effort to rebuild streets, water and sewer systems and buildings to accommodate the influx of gamblers created inconvenience. Dust, noise and local traffic congestion were of a scale never imagined or previously experienced by local residents.

Safety and Security. When asked about their perceptions regarding safety and security, respondents from both states felt that they personally, their families and their homes and possessions were safe, although Colorado respondents felt slightly less so than Deadwood respondents. (See Figure 13.)

Figure 13: Perceived Changes in Safety and Security

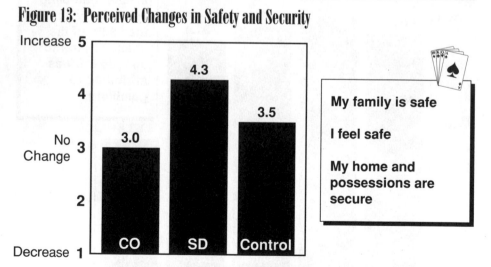

Score indicates the overall average of the individual average response to the three referenced questions.

Residents in every community felt that the number of serious crimes had increased—and that this could be attributed to gambling. (See Figure 14.)

Statistics provided by the Deadwood City Police Department indicate that crime has indeed risen substantially since gambling began. In 1989, calls to the police department for service totaled 1,483. By 1992, this number had more than doubled to 3,207. Most of this increase is reflected in increases in traffic and criminal offenses. But driving while intoxicated (DWI) offenses increased only slightly over the same period, going from 74 in 1989 to 89 in 1992. Juvenile offenses rose from 36 in 1989 to 76 in 1990, but tapered off again to 38 by 1992.

The number of law enforcement officers increased from five in 1989 to 10 in 1992, and the police department budget increased from $185,000 in 1989 to $472,000 in 1992. There was also a corresponding increase in the number of police vehicles and the amount of training provided to officers. It is clear, however, that a significantly increased law enforcement presence was caused mostly by increases in the sheer number of visitors to Deadwood due to gambling.

Residents in every community felt that the number of serious crimes had increased

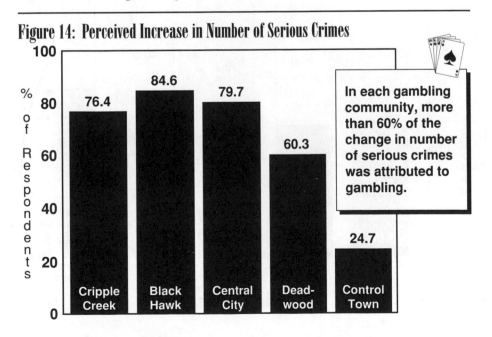

Figure 14: Perceived Increase in Number of Serious Crimes

% of Respondents

- Cripple Creek: 76.4
- Black Hawk: 84.6
- Central City: 79.7
- Deadwood: 60.3
- Control Town: 24.7

In each gambling community, more than 60% of the change in number of serious crimes was attributed to gambling.

More than 45 percent of the residents in each gambling community perceive a negative change in their ability to influence local government decisions

In Black Hawk (population 227), the massive influx of gamblers also led to major change in law enforcement and crime. The police force, non-existent prior to gambling, today consists of a staff of 22. The town now has a budget in excess of $1 million—comparable to that of a city of 15,000. Cripple Creek's police department has increased from three officers in 1991 to 24 today. And, in Central City, after one year of gambling, total reported crimes increased from 72 to 586. Thefts were up from 34 to 145, drunken driving offenses up from 29 to 83, public intoxication up from 12 to 115, and liquor violations up from 3 to 52. Some of this documented increase is certainly due to stricter enforcement and reporting.

Influence on Local Politics. More than 45 percent of the residents in each gambling community indicated they perceive a negative change in their ability to influence local government decisions. Respondents feel they have less political influence now than before gambling. (See Figure 15.)

Figure 15: Perceived Change in Influence over Local Government Decisions

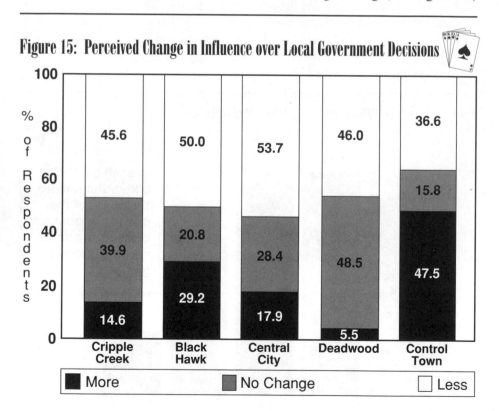

They also perceive that the gambling industry has greater influence than individual citizens on council decisions generally, on council decisions that influence gambling, on city budget decisions and on decisions regarding construction and use of public facilities. (See Figure 16.)

Figure 16: Resident Perception of Political Influence

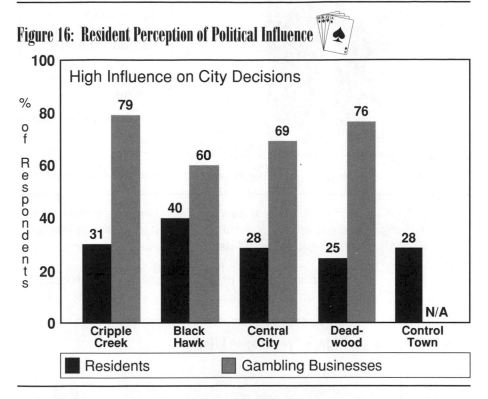

Historic Preservation and Cultural Exchange. Residents from both states expressed strong agreement about the value of historic preservation. Both Colorado and Deadwood residents were in firm agreement that it was important that their communities maintain their National Historic Landmark status and preserve the town's history. (See Figure 17.)

But despite this strong indication of importance of restoration and preservation, Colorado residents perceived no change in the efforts to restore or protect historic buildings and provide historic activities and programs. (See Figure 18.) By contrast, residents of Deadwood

Figure 17: Importance of Historic Preservation

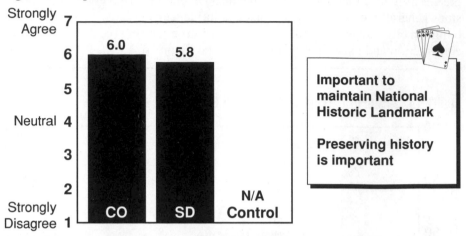

Score indicates the overall average of the individual average response to the two referenced questions.

strongly felt they were seeing improvement in the restoration and protection of historical buildings and an increase in the availability of historical activities and programs.

Regarding cultural exchange, residents in both states felt that the opportunities to meet interesting people and to

Figure 18: Community Historic Preservation Efforts

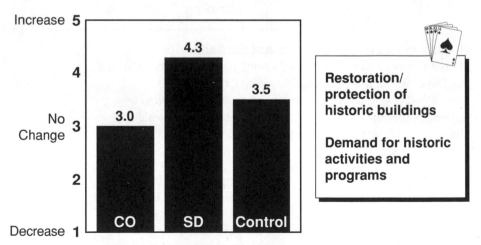

Score indicates the overall average of the individual average response to the two referenced questions.

learn about other people and cultures had increased, although only slightly in the Colorado towns.

Deadwood residents' more positive response in assessing local historic preservation efforts may be tied to the fact that 100 percent of the state gambling tax revenue returned to the city is used for historic restoration and preservation. A liberal interpretation of what constitutes historic preservation has allowed Deadwood to spend millions of dollars on everything from restoring museums to improving the street, water and sewer systems. Also, $1 million was spent to refurbish the city's recreation center, which had been built as a public auditorium in 1912.

Another example of Deadwood's historic development initiative is the establishment of a $2 million low-interest revolving loan fund. This fund has supported the restoration of both the Bullock and Fairmont Hotels. In addition, the rehabilitation of the Gilmore Hotel into low- and moderate-income housing was funded at a half-million dollars. To date, 27 low-interest commercial property loans and 17 residential loans have been made. In addition, funding has been provided to paint historic houses, to establish a creek trail and to provide walking tour signs.

Efforts to restore and preserve historic structures in the Colorado gambling towns have not been as extensive or effective as those in Deadwood

Efforts to restore and preserve historic structures in the Colorado gambling towns have not been as extensive or effective as those in Deadwood. The interpretation of what constitutes historic preservation in Colorado is limited and the amount of money dedicated to restoration and preservation is much less than that received by Deadwood. With few exceptions, only the facades of buildings remodeled for use as casinos remain historically intact. Residents seem to be questioning the integrity of their vote for gambling as a means to preserve the history of their community.

Economic Impact

In both states, residents perceived a substantial increase in the revenue generated in the local economy, in jobs and personal income of local residents, and in the amount of income going to local businesses. (See Figure 19.) They also indicated agreement with statements that local property taxes, sales tax and cost of living had increased.

Figure 19: Perceived Changes in Local Economy

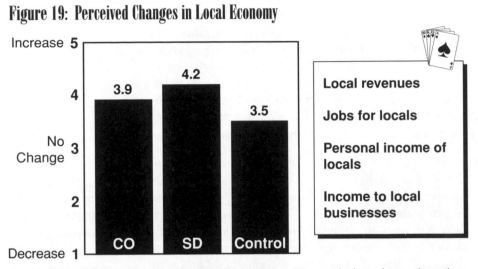

Score indicates the overall average of the individual average response to the four referenced questions.

Commercial and Residential Property. In Deadwood, although there had been some movement in the real estate market in the fall of 1988 prior to November 1, the immediate success of gambling touched off a flurry of real estate transactions. Buildings that only months before had a fair market value of less than $100,000 were now being listed and sold for a $1 million or more.

Buildings that only months before had a fair market value of less than $100,000 were now being listed and sold for a $1 million or more

Within the following year, approximately 90 percent of the commercial property in Deadwood had been converted to gambling, resulting in the licensing of over 80 casinos. Not all casinos have been successful, however. To date, nine gambling properties have closed. With few exceptions a majority of the other commercial establishments, such as hardware, clothing, car dealerships and other retail enterprises, were purchased and converted to gambling.

In Colorado, although there had been speculative real estate transactions during the early stages of the initiative process, once gambling was formally approved, the value of commercial property jumped dramatically. One casino property increased in value from less than $20 per square foot prior to approval of gambling to $560 per square foot after gambling was approved. Commercial property taxes have increased accordingly.

Although not true in all of the gambling communities, residential property in Black Hawk and Central City has experienced a substantial decline in property taxes while increasing in valuation. One $57,000 residence has experienced a decrease in property tax from $1,500 to less than $300 over the past three years. Total assessed valuation of Gilpin County has increased since gambling from $33 million to $117 million, with Central City's property tax assessment dropping 99.4 percent and Black Hawk's by 83 percent.

Employment. Residents' perception that employment opportunities in the gambling towns have increased is supported by data collected from the Colorado Department of Labor. A recent department publication indicated that "the [services] industry . . . got a boost from the expansion of limited stakes gaming facilities in Teller and Gilpin counties. The net addition of 5,200 workers within the amusement and recreation subsector reflects this gambling related hiring."[10] Further, these jobs are mostly in casinos and restaurants, which provide opportunities for both adults and young people.

Figures show that the total labor force in both the Colorado counties remained relatively constant from 1985 to 1990, jumped slightly in 1991 and then made substantial gains in 1992. In 1992, Gilpin County added almost 1,100 jobs to a 1991 base of 1,800 workers, at the same time keeping the unemployment rate constant and low at 4.4 percent. Because labor participation rates in tourism-dependent towns normally swell during the high season, the summer of 1993 should produce the highest figures in the past two decades.

Despite the substantial increase in jobs, it is unclear how many residents of the gambling towns are now actually employed in gambling. In order for gambling to

Despite the substantial increase in jobs, it is unclear how many residents of the gambling towns are now actually employed in gambling

positively impact a community's employment opportunities, the types of jobs and subsequent salaries must match residents' employment and salary needs. In Colorado, as casinos replaced stores and businesses in the gambling communities, what few traditional jobs existed were lost. Many of the entry-level positions in casinos offered a pay scale similar to the jobs that were lost.

Many of the entry-level positions in casinos offered a pay scale similar to the jobs that were lost

In addition, one elected official in Colorado noted that long-term residents who sought tranquility and isolation when they moved to the community find it difficult to work in a casino with excessive noise, light, people and congestion. These employees have been known to quit or to be among the first let go when cutbacks are made, because they have trouble adjusting to the work environment.

A March 1991 report prepared by University of South Dakota economics professor Dr. Michael Madden looked at three major economic impact variables—expenditures, employment and earnings—and at fiscal impacts after one year of gambling in Deadwood.[11] Madden reported that Deadwood had received 67.2 percent ($9.1 million) of the $13,581,038 increase in taxable sales for eating and drinking and lodging establishments in the three major cities located in Lawrence County.

Madden estimated the number of new gambling-related employees throughout the first year of gambling to be 1,030 and the amount of new earnings received by workers connected to the Deadwood gambling industry to be $14,570,000. He also found that the first 12 months of gambling produced nearly $6.4 million from gaming taxes for special historical projects and that city sales tax receipts increased by 73 percent. In addition, he suggested that the property tax base on commercial property that was scheduled for reappraisal could increase by a factor of three to five times, resulting in an increase in new property taxes for local governments of up to $1.7 million.

In a December 1992 update, Madden reported that at least $32 million in construction costs associated with building permits had taken place in Deadwood in conjunction with the gambling industry. He also reported that the average employment in direct visitor sectors had approached 3,000 workers in Lawrence County and that $17.4 million in new earnings had been received by workers connected with the Deadwood gambling industry.

Social Service Impact

Survey respondents were not specifically asked about their perceptions of social services, or about the homeless and disenfranchised populations that receive those services. However, data collected from state and local social service agencies in both states provide insight into social impacts that may affect residents' perceptions of community life.

Local, county and state social services officials in the Colorado towns, as well as in Deadwood, generally agreed that financial assistance programs such as Aid to Families with Dependent Children (AFDC), Supplemental Security Income, Food Stamps and Low Income Energy Assistance have either remained constant or have seen a decrease in average enrollments.

In fact, AFDC cases in Gilpin County (which includes Central City and Black Hawk) have remained relatively constant with some seasonal fluctuations since gambling began. There has even been some slight decrease in the average number of monthly recipients during the first year of gambling. Information on AFDC caseloads in Teller County (which includes Cripple Creek) and Lawrence County (which includes Deadwood) saw similar trends. Lawrence County experienced a net loss of Food Stamp recipients since gambling began, dropping from 436 in 1989 to 403 in 1992, and dipping just under 400 for the two years in between.

AFDC cases in Gilpin County have remained relatively constant with some seasonal fluctuations since gambling began

Child protection and other social service programs, on the other hand, have seen increases since gambling started. In recent years, youth and child neglect cases have been recognized as public problems rather than as private family matters. Despite this shift and the greater awareness of and willingness to report such cases, the data clearly show a sustained increase in youth-related, child protection and domestic abuse counseling programs. In Central City, child protection cases increased sixfold from May 1991 (prior to gambling) to May 1992.

In the service providers' judgment, the differences between financial programs and service programs stem from two main factors. First, the availability of jobs and higher entry wages has decreased residents' dependence on government-provided financial assistance. Second, increases in time spent away from the home, traffic congestion and the number of visitors have created a more stressful environment, which can have impacts on child protection and domestic and substance abuse.

Although real changes in health care services have been relatively slight in all the gambling towns, the three Colorado towns did add to their emergency and ambulatory medical capacities. Deadwood's changes in health care since gambling have been negligible mostly because a full-service hospital (Northern Hills General Hospital) with 35 beds and 11 physicians already existed prior to gambling. Next door to the hospital is the Black Hills Medical Center, which sees patients on an outpatient basis, with six full-time and two part-time physicians. None of the Colorado towns has a full-service medical facility, much less a hospital.

Increases in time spent away from the home, traffic congestion and the number of visitors have created a more stressful environment, which can have impacts on child protection and domestic and substance abuse

Community Life Impact

Quality of Life. The residents in Deadwood and the Colorado towns expressed different feelings about the quality of life in their community. Of those responding to the survey, Black Hawk and Deadwood residents expressed the greatest satisfaction—50 percent and 51 percent, respectively, while Cripple Creek and Central City residents expressed strong dissatisfaction—53 percent and 65 percent, respectively. (See Figure 20.)

At the time this survey was conducted, residents from Central City (76%) and Cripple Creek (56%) expressed strong disagreement with the statement "My town is an

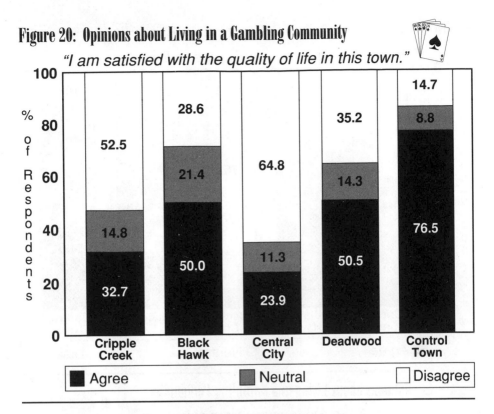

Figure 20: Opinions about Living in a Gambling Community

"I am satisfied with the quality of life in this town."

% of Respondents

	Cripple Creek	Black Hawk	Central City	Deadwood	Control Town
Disagree	52.5	28.6	64.8	35.2	14.7
Neutral	14.8	21.4	11.3	14.3	8.8
Agree	32.7	50.0	23.9	50.5	76.5

■ Agree   ▦ Neutral   □ Disagree

ideal place to live." About 40 percent of residents from both Deadwood and Black Hawk also disagreed strongly with this statement. (See Figure 21.)

When asked whether they would like to move away from their community, 44 percent of the Cripple Creek residents, 32 percent of Black Hawk residents, 39 percent of Central City residents and 29 percent of Deadwood residents said they would consider moving. (See Figure 22.)

Residents of the Colorado towns indicated no change in the quality of recreation opportunities, in the variety of social opportunities, in the life and vitality of the town or in the variety of cultural facilities and activities. Deadwood residents indicated there had been a slight increase. Residents of both states indicated a dramatic increase in the variety of both restaurants and entertainment, although they had experienced a significant decrease in the variety of retail shopping outlets.

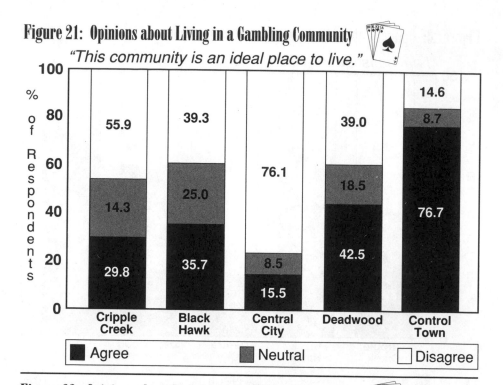

Figure 21: Opinions about Living in a Gambling Community

"This community is an ideal place to live."

Cripple Creek: Agree 29.8, Neutral 14.3, Disagree 55.9
Black Hawk: Agree 35.7, Neutral 25.0, Disagree 39.3
Central City: Agree 15.5, Neutral 8.5, Disagree 76.1
Deadwood: Agree 42.5, Neutral 18.5, Disagree 39.0
Control Town: Agree 76.7, Neutral 8.7, Disagree 14.6

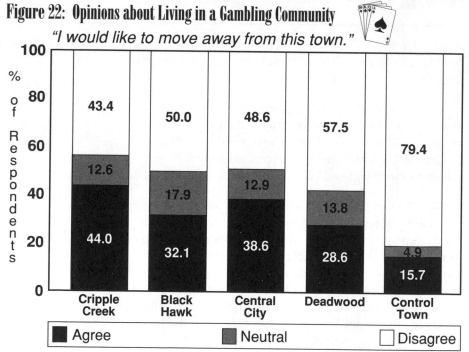

Figure 22: Opinions about Living in a Gambling Community

"I would like to move away from this town."

Cripple Creek: Agree 44.0, Neutral 12.6, Disagree 43.4
Black Hawk: Agree 32.1, Neutral 17.9, Disagree 50.0
Central City: Agree 38.6, Neutral 12.9, Disagree 48.6
Deadwood: Agree 28.6, Neutral 13.8, Disagree 57.5
Control Town: Agree 15.7, Neutral 4.9, Disagree 79.4

Regarding the quality of the natural environment, Colorado residents perceived a decrease and Deadwood residents perceived no change. When assessing changes in government services (police, fire, medical), all residents indicated only a slight increase in the ability of such services to meet demand, in the quality of such services and in the financial resources available for services.

Gambling: Yes or No? Although 54 percent of the residents from the Colorado towns and 68 percent of the residents from Deadwood voted for gambling in their respective statewide referenda, only five percent of the Colorado residents and 10 percent of the Deadwood residents indicated they would recommend that other towns legalize gambling. Fifty-nine percent of the Colorado residents and 34 percent of the Deadwood residents said they would not recommend such action. Thirty-seven percent of the Colorado residents and 56 percent of the Deadwood residents said it depended presumably on whether the community understood the consequences and was adequately prepared.

Only five percent of the Colorado residents and 10 percent of the Deadwood residents indicated they would recommend that other towns legalize gambling

Generally, Deadwood respondents expressed greater satisfaction with the status of gambling in their community than did Colorado respondents. Several possible reasons might explain this difference: Deadwood residents have had more time to adjust to the changes that have occurred. Deadwood has a larger population base and geographic size and, thus, may be better able to accommodate the many changes. Necessary daily services are still available in Deadwood or nearby. State policy in South Dakota is generally more supportive of gambling. And finally, greater financial resources are being dedicated to local infrastructure development in Deadwood.

Response from the Comparison Community. Responses from residents of Grand Lake, a non-gambling community, offer an interesting comparison and additional insight into the responses of residents from the gambling communities. Grand Lake is also experiencing tremendous change due to its rapidly emerging tourism industry. Much like Deadwood and the Colorado gambling towns, with this growth in tourism, Grand Lake has experienced a 44-percent increase in sales tax revenues this calendar year and a 33-percent increase in sales tax revenues this fiscal year. Residents indicated that they, too, perceived increases in crowding and congestion and in the number of serious crimes. They also feel that their ability to influence local government decisions has decreased over the past three years.

But residents of Grand Lake did express greater general satisfaction with life in their community. They indicated a greater sense of safety and security, community involvement, community affiliation and the desire to preserve history. They do not feel they would benefit socially or economically from gambling; they do not support gambling in their town; and they feel they would lose both traditional tourists and current residents if gambling were initiated.

Concerns of Casino and Local Government Officials

Once state approval is given for gambling it should be recognized as a legitimate business

Once state approval is given for gambling it should be recognized as a legitimate business. Thus, an environment should be created that provides full opportunity for its success. Yet this has not happened with small town gambling.

Casino owners and managers, easily targeted as the "bad guys," are conducting legitimate business but within an uncertain economic and political climate. Government officials who once made their important but somewhat limited political decisions in a rather casual environment suddenly have found themselves in a highly political and stressful decisionmaking situation.

To better understand the perspective and needs of the gambling industry, focus groups were conducted with casino owners and managers from Black Hawk, Central City and Deadwood. Casino owners from both states expressed similar goals and encountered similar problems, but their reactions to what they experienced reflected interesting differences.

As might be expected, casino owners want first and foremost to make a profit. But, in conjunction with that, they want to be recognized for their significant contribution to the economy and to be treated fairly. Owners from both states expressed concern that they had not done a good job of educating people about their economic contributions or about the risks they bear. They also felt they were not recognized for their social contribution to the community. Things such as renovation of both historic and other commercial buildings, the creation of thousands of jobs, their local purchasing practices, self-policing in the casinos, support of special events for the communities and the attraction of additional tourist dollars were all seen as undervalued contributions.

Casino owners want to be recognized for their significant contribution to the economy and to be treated fairly

In dealing with state government, casino owners expressed a desire for a governor who would be neutral and fair; a legislature that would be educated about the industry and enlightened about running business; and a gaming commission that understood business generally, understood the industry in particular and was willing to work with the industry.

Owners discussed many problems they faced in getting started. The size of the front-end investment was cited as substantial, at least partly due to state policy. The advanced payments of licenses and fees, level of taxation, building safety standards, number of allowable machines and the availability of front-end incentives were all factors in the size of investment required. These state policy-related costs add to the more fixed costs, such as acquiring property, renovating buildings and paying employees.

Owners and town officials had similar views about the initial problems. The lack of advance planning, unwillingness of neighboring communities to work with each other for the common good, the fears and suspicions about the industry and owners, the inadequacy of the infrastructure, the delay in having money to work with and the rapid escalation in numbers of establishments and people coming to gamble were all mentioned as serious problems.

These two groups also tended to agree that it was probably unrealistic to think that gambling would stay a small adjunct attraction to existing businesses. They agreed that an equitable distribution of monies to all the critical parties, including schools, would benefit them all. And they claimed that retail business was closing down because of competition from Wal-Mart and regional shopping centers, not because of the introduction of gambling.

Colorado casino owners had more specific criticism of state and local officials than South Dakota casino owners did. Because they were not allowed to run for local political office, Colorado gambling representatives feel that city officials listen to residents more than to the industry. Thus, they feel disenfranchised with local politics. They also feel disenfranchised by not having direct representation on the state tourism board. Currently in South Dakota, one member of the tourism advisory board is a casino owner. Proposed policy would establish a formal appointment for a representative from the gambling industry.

Colorado casino owners also gave a number of examples of ways they felt the state was putting up roadblocks or at least not being helpful. In particular, they felt the state was changing the rules of the game by raising tax rates and device fees after owners' investments had been made.

When asked "Would you do it again?" the South Dakota owners' response was, "In a heartbeat"

Although owners from both states lamented what they saw as unnecessary adversarial relations with government, particularly in getting started, the Colorado group clearly was more troubled by it. When asked "Would you do it again?" the South Dakota owners' response was, "In a heartbeat." Colorado owners, however, talked about alternative business opportunities on reservations, with riverboats or in other lines of business.

Chapter 5. Understanding the Game

Gambling means many things to different people: a source of entertainment and a chance to "win the jackpot" for the consumer, the possibility of a dramatic increase in real estate values for the commercial business owner, a source of untapped tax revenue for the state legislator, a job for the poker dealer. Gambling is all of these and much more.

Policymakers often feel ambivalent about gambling. On the one hand there are good arguments against gambling because of moral issues and the social problems associated with it. Yet, the economic benefits are so great that they seem to outweigh the moral and social arguments. People are tired of tax increases, yet don't want public services to decrease. Gambling provides an alternative.

Policymakers often feel ambivalent about gambling

This ambivalence poses several dilemmas for the state in terms of how it should respond and how it can balance these concerns. The first dilemma is whether to deal with gambling reactively or proactively. Dilemma two is how to balance regulation, mitigation and promotion. The third dilemma is whether to view the revenues as a dependable source of funding or as a windfall.

This chapter provides an overview of the governance of gambling in American society, outlines these dilemmas in more detail and sets the stage for the ensuing discussion of state policy considerations.

Gambling: The Historical Context

Over its long and varied history in the United States, gambling generally has been viewed as both an economic and a moral issue. Economically, the traditional question has been, "How can we use gambling to generate dollars for profit and economic development?" Morally, the intensity of citizens' responses to gambling has ranged from the anti-gambling moralists who smashed card tables with sledge hammers to those who saw gambling as a natural part of the Wild West.

But gambling is also fundamentally a political issue because of its inextricable link with governance. Historically, gambling has been used by government to fund projects such as the Jamestown settlement, Ivy League universities and the Continental Army, in addition to being used to meet many local needs.

While these early projects were funded by unregulated lotteries, today's lotteries typically are monopolies run by states for profit. States justify their lotteries by returning only about half the proceeds as prizes, with the remaining monies going to state treasuries, sometimes dedicated for "public" purposes.

In order to generate higher revenues, states actively advertise their lotteries, encouraging citizens to play because it's fun and a public-spirited thing to do. Lotteries can be marketed in such fashion because they are seen as substantially different from casino gambling, which traditionally connoted private profit, liquor, the opportunity for infiltration by organized crime, weak-willed gamblers losing their life savings, and professional gamblers taking advantage of honest working folk.

The broad use and acceptance of lotteries clearly have paved the way for the expansion of gambling to many other forms

Whether desired or not, the broad use and acceptance of lotteries clearly have paved the way for the expansion of gambling to many other forms, including casino gambling. The city of New Orleans, which is limiting casino gambling to one heavily regulated establishment, may be the closest to operating a casino like a lottery.

Over time, American society has been socialized to gambling. The evolution of lotteries and Nevada's 1931 legalization of gambling have familiarized Americans with the benefits and pitfalls of gambling. Without the gradual exposure to gambling and without evidence of economic windfalls, America probably would not be so receptive to the idea of legalized gambling today.

Gambling is rapidly becoming explicitly condoned throughout America and a more liberal, positive attitude toward it is prevailing. History tells us that ideas and social/political change tend to move fairly slowly at first, picking up speed the more the activity or attitude becomes commonplace in society. With gambling becoming commonplace, it is helping shape our political and moral framework.

Arguments Against Gambling

The public tolerance for gambling is tested every time new or expanded gambling is proposed. While many citizens are neutral or support gambling, opponents inevitably appear. During the 1990 debate on allowing gambling in Colorado, the opponents' basic moral argument was that gambling hinders the moral progress of society, and that, because of adverse effects on the socialization process (especially upon youth), it should be restricted.

Political columnist George Will supports this view when he writes that "gambling inflames the lust for wealth without work, weakening a perishable American belief—that the moral worth of a person is gauged not by how much money he makes but by how he makes his money."[12]

Traditional opposition to gambling also has come from those who fear the infiltration of organized crime. But Dr. William Eadington argues that "as legal commercial gambling has become more legitimate and established, and as regulatory bodies have become more professional and sophisticated, the opportunities for corruption and for organized crime infiltration into gambling operations have diminished."[13]

It would seem to follow that if gambling remains "clean," opposition would decline. That may not necessarily be the case, however

It would seem to follow that if gambling remains "clean," opposition would decline. That may not necessarily be the case, however, if one considers the results of recent initiatives to further expand gambling in South Dakota and Colorado. The arguments against gambling presented in Colorado's "Analysis of 1992 Ballot Proposals" prepared by the Legislative Council of the Colorado

State Legislature, state that "the quality of life appreciated by Colorado residents and visitors will be threatened by the continued expansion of gambling throughout the state. More gambling will lead to increased social problems, alcohol-related accidents, traffic violations, crime, and gambling addiction." These arguments prevailed. The ballot proposals were defeated overwhelmingly.

Gambling creates moral and social issues for society, one of which is addictive gambling

There is no doubt that gambling creates moral and social issues for society, one of which is addictive gambling. In recent years, with many new forms of gambling becoming legal in a large number of states, gambling addiction, with its accompanying social and moral ills, has become a major area of study.

Though there apparently is no consensus about whether or not gambling is a physiologically addictive behavior, gambling addiction—or "problem gambling"—is a societal concern. The long-term implications and costs associated with rehabilitation and the educational programs necessary to mitigate the problem cannot be ignored.

Gambling and Economics

The current wave of pro-gambling sentiment clearly has risen on the heels of increasing fiscal constraints at the state and local levels coupled with an increase in demand on government to provide services. The potential for increases in jobs, tax revenues, real estate investments and general economic and community enhancement makes gambling attractive.

In her recent book *Reviving the American Dream,* Alice Rivlin states that ". . . government will probably face continuing fiscal stress in the 1990s. Policies to revitalize the economy—increased public investment, a federal surplus, health financing reform—cannot be undertaken without more revenue at some level of government. The public seems angry and dissatisfied with government, however, and unwilling either to increase its support or to accept a lower level of services."[14]

Despite the fact that Rivlin is talking generally about the condition of the national economy, her points relate well to all levels of government. In many respects, we as a society seem to have reached the peak of our willingness to pay for government services. Gambling has arisen as one alternative to either raising taxes or decreasing public services, or both.

Gambling, however, seems very vulnerable to the economic conditions of the times. The cycles of gambling in the United States indicate that during hard economic times we are more open to ideas, such as gambling, that otherwise would not be considered; yet when prosperity reigns, we are quick to cast off gambling as morally degenerative. Morality could be characterized as a luxury to be afforded during the good times. Clearly, the acceptability of gambling depends on our current societal values, which are shaped in part by prevailing economic conditions.

When prosperity reigns, we are quick to cast off gambling as morally degenerative

States' Dilemmas

Government at all levels gets caught in the tug of war between morality, social impact and economic benefits. Several dilemmas result.

♠ **Dilemma 1: Should states be reactive or proactive?** A very important factor influencing the way the political system accepts gambling is the way gambling is initiated. Casino gambling can be legalized through various political means. State policy is developed reactively or proactively, depending upon whether gambling is brought in through a citizens' initiative or by vote of the state legislature.

South Dakota and Colorado both experienced a grassroots movement, forcing government to deal with gambling reactively. Local communities pressed the state to seek economic enhancement. Most other state governments, however, embraced gambling to raise state tax revenues, an approach one Colorado official termed "entrepreneurship."

This distinction between reactive and proactive responses to gambling is very important when one considers the obligations of state government and the enthusiasm of decisionmakers. The result can have a strong influence on state policy.

♠ **Dilemma 2: How can the state address conflicting concerns as it regulates gambling?** In the decades and even centuries that this nation has struggled with the acceptability of gambling, government has played a variety of roles—from prohibiting gambling to encouraging it, offering it as a government monopoly and regulating it as a private business venture. The legacy of widely varied and contradictory roles, together with the rationale that supports each role, contributes to the confusion and uncertainty that characterize state policy toward gambling.

The result of the ambivalence about moral objections and economic benefits is that lawmakers address the negative social and moral consequences of gambling through a series of regulatory strictures that attempt to minimize the adverse impacts on society. Ironically, these conflicting regulations can threaten the very economic success of the industry.

♠ **Dilemma 3: How should the state use gambling revenues?** The newfound source of revenue generated by gambling raises several questions about how state and local governments should handle the money gambling brings in. First, at what point should government begin to depend on gambling revenues as a consistent source of income? This question is a source of considerable concern for anyone familiar with state budgeting. If states begin to use gambling revenues for important long-term programs, such as entitlement programs, prisons, education or debt reduction, they are placing the state at the mercy of a very cyclical and untested industry.

If states begin to use gambling revenues for important long-term programs, they are placing the state at the mercy of a very cyclical and untested industry

This leaves relatively few areas within government where gambling revenues may be used appropriately. Unable to consider entitlement programs, other important long-term programs and long-term debt reduction, governments are left with one-time capital project financing, short-term deficit reduction and other "non-essential" programs that otherwise would not get funded in times of economic stagnation. These may include socially redeeming programs that can counter some of the opposition to gambling.

One may argue that the problems gambling generates outweigh the benefits of funding non-essential programs, such as historic preservation, that are generally far down the state's priority list. However, the state's economic well-being is not tied solely to revenues. Bottom-line considerations also must include new jobs that are created, new income and commercial taxes that are collected, and new business development that is spawned. All of these factors figure prominently in the decisionmaking quandary.

Bottom line considerations also must include new jobs, new income and commercial taxes, and new business development

In light of the dilemmas policymakers face, how can governments make the best decisions? The next chapter examines more closely state strategies for dealing with gambling.

Chapter 6. Raising the Stakes: State Policy Issues

This chapter draws on experiences from South Dakota, Colorado and other states in formulating strategic questions states must ask as they determine their stance on gambling and develop any gambling policies they might adopt. Concerns relating to state policies focus on regulation, revenues, economic development and social impacts. Since the best way to deal with all four areas is through thoughtful planning, a special section is included that deals with planning considerations specific to casino gambling.

Regulation

Regulating gambling is perhaps the most straightforward and comfortable role for states, and most states emphasize the regulatory function above all others. Regulation is important because it protects the integrity of the games, ensuring that cheating and fraud do not occur. It also ensures that revenues are collected and distributed according to reputable practices and that criminal elements are kept out. Gambling commissions establish and oversee the regulatory process. Regulation of gambling includes:

Regulating gambling is perhaps the most straightforward and comfortable role for states

♣ issuing licenses according to law

♣ limiting the variety of games, stakes, losses, numbers of machines and tables, level of payout, floor space, liquor availability, hours, location and other factors.

The regulatory process also includes enforcing regulations through:

♦ conducting background checks of owners, operators, employees, equipment distributors and suppliers

♦ conducting both on-site and off-site enforcement

♦ performing audits of business operations.

Overly onerous regulations or taxation levels not only can weaken the casino operations, they may in fact create some of the problems they are designed to avoid

Initially, states are very concerned that gambling not tarnish the state's reputation, and state personnel may be inclined to be very restrictive to ensure the integrity of the industry. A state may want to make certain it is not perceived as soft on crime or open to "sin" pursuits and, thus, may throw the "regulatory book" at casinos. However, experience tells us that states need to balance regulatory firmness with maintaining a viable industry. Overly onerous regulations or taxation levels not only can weaken the casino operations and/or drive them to other locations, they may in fact create some of the problems they are designed to avoid.

For example, as mentioned earlier, 22 Colorado casinos have failed. Colorado's high tax rate and other regulatory requirements appear to have helped drive out smaller operators, forcing some casino owners to expand to pay costs or to sell to outside "deep pockets" that had enough resources to meet the demands. South Dakota, on the other hand, took the position of recognizing the financial conditions and needs of the industry, but insisted upon compliance with established regulations and internal control procedures.

As the gambling industry matures, however, it may become more difficult to stay "regulatory neutral." Because of growing competition nationwide and the economics of the industry, pressure has built to expand the limits—higher stakes, more variety of games, additional locations and larger operations. As states become accustomed to gambling and recognize the benefits in terms of jobs, revenues and economically revived communities, commissions and elected officials find it increasingly difficult to resist helping the hometown industry.

Revenues

Revenue collection and distribution is closely tied to regulation. As the gambling industry is getting established, the pattern of revenue collection among states varies widely.

Revenue Collection. Revenue collection refers to the amount and ways that monies are taken in by the relevant government jurisdictions. Money is collected through various taxes and fees. The AGP tax is taken "off the top" before operating expenses, representing the largest source of state revenue.

At least four levels of government feel the impact: cities, counties, schools and the state. But no state in our survey has built all four into the revenue process. The state typically plays the largest role in collecting revenues, with cities having a smaller role with their collection of device fees, parking fees and riverboat boarding fees. Counties and schools usually must depend on the increase in property values or on their share of money distributed by the state.

If a state and the community don't coordinate, taxation levels may become more than the industry can absorb. Colorado has had a 20-percent tax rate on casino earnings over $1 million, plus application and license fees, in addition to a device fee of $150. Local communities are allowed to add their own device fees which, in the case of Cripple Creek, is an additional $1,200. Fees also are assessed to provide local parking. The combination of these taxes and fees has caused some casinos to reduce the number of machines they operate.

If a state and the community don't coordinate, taxation levels may become more than the industry can absorb

In addition to the direct levies on the industry, government tax revenues related to gambling are likely to increase from a wide range of other sources, including income taxes, increased property tax revenues, new investments and sales taxes. Although all the studied jurisdictions that offered limited-stakes casino gambling have experienced an initial increase in sales tax revenues, it is simply too early to determine what long-term patterns will be and how they will influence revenues.

Nelson Rose of the Whittier School of Law argues that these early successes with generating revenue are a result of pent-up demand: When the market becomes saturated, many owners and governments may be left with either new operations that can't make it or with established operations that can't stay competitive. In particular, he warns of problems for rural areas that may be difficult to get to, smaller operations that can't afford to upgrade or operations in areas that don't have other attractions to help draw tourists.[15]

Revenue Distribution. The distribution of revenues raises other issues. Gambling often is sold to voters as a way to pay for socially desirable ends. Colorado's lottery was sold as a way to pay for parks and wildlife. South Dakota sold gambling in Deadwood as a way to achieve historic preservation. Illinois directs money to education, while New Jersey funds services for seniors and the disabled. In reality, most states put the lion's share into the general fund.

All four state and local levels of government should benefit financially if local services are to remain in balance and hard feelings are to be avoided

There are several caveats regarding distribution. All four state and local levels of government should benefit financially if local services are to remain in balance and hard feelings are to be avoided. Deadwood, where the bulk of the revenues is designated for historic preservation and restoration, offers an extreme example. However, to spread the benefits as widely as possible in Deadwood, historic preservation has been broadly interpreted to include water and sewer systems, fire service and anything else that contributes to historic preservation.

Indeed, because of the increase in property valuation, the Lead-Deadwood school district has lost out on a portion of its state funding through the state equalization formula. Local property taxes will catch up, but for several years the imbalance will cause financial hardship and potential ill feelings. Schools do qualify for and have received grants through the local historic preservation fund to restore their historic buildings and do history-related projects.

Similarly, Colorado authorized funding for impacts to contiguous counties, but no impact mitigation funds have been made available for the gambling communities. Although the Department of Local Affairs was authorized to provide $75,000 for each of three years to each of the respective counties for planning, this commitment was rescinded after one year. In addition, gambling revenues paid to the state for redistribution to the local communities weren't distributed for almost a year after gambling began. Thus, for that time period, the gambling communities were left to prepare as best they could with limited financial resources and an overwhelming agenda of needs.

Many community residents not connected with the gambling industry feel they are the ones left holding the bag

Many community residents not connected with the gambling industry feel they are the ones left holding the bag. They must deal with all the negative social impacts of gambling but receive none of the economic benefits. To compensate for this perception, it is recommended that gambling tax revenues be used to provide funding for quality of life improvements for the community—improved streets, water and sewer; better social services; recreation centers, new parks, senior services, community festivals and similar purposes.

Deadwood has refurbished its community recreation facility and expanded the number of community events. In addition, grants to nonprofits such as churches (including Baptist, Methodist, Episcopal and Catholic), schools and social organizations (for example, Masons) have touched the lives of most residents in some positive way.

Black Hawk and Central City have signed a memorandum of understanding with Gilpin County to support parks and recreation development, but have made only limited progress due to other spending priorities. Cripple Creek offers limited summer youth programs.

The question of who benefits from the distribution of revenues created by gambling is an important one. It continues to call for the thoughtful design of gambling initiatives.

Gambling as Economic Development

Both South Dakota and Colorado introduced gambling through the citizen initiative process. The result in both cases was an initial defensive posture on the part of the state—that is, "How do we keep gambling from causing problems and bad public relations?" However, more than half the states surveyed launched gambling as a legislative initiative, most because they saw it as an opportunity for economic development and a source of new revenues.

States have many programs to attract and benefit new industry—tax breaks, special zoning, training programs, inclusion of industry officials on civic boards, assistance with bonding, marketing help and a host of others. The gambling industry is treated differently.

If gambling is to be more than simply tolerated as an economic development strategy, there are serious implications for state policy. For one thing, states must recognize that the gambling industry itself is undergoing fundamental change. Because of the growth in gambling worldwide, the industry is becoming much more competitive. This means that to attract business, casinos may have to upgrade their appearance, offer quality food and entertainment, provide sleeping rooms or campgrounds, furnish child care or other activities to entertain children and, in general, help communities become desirable draws.

Highly restrictive regulations, heavy taxes and punitive attitudes can limit the ability of casino owners to respond to competitive needs

Highly restrictive regulations, heavy taxes and punitive attitudes can limit the ability of casino owners to respond to competitive needs. Even laissez-faire policies may make it difficult to take advantage of the economic benefits that gambling can bring. While not actively promoting gambling, states can still assist with attracting related amenities, such as employee housing, child care activities, local beautification and the coordination of varied state services for the community's general development.

In general, states should consider carefully what they can do to contribute to integrating gambling with existing development so that both stay healthy. New Orleans provides an interesting example. The Louisiana State Legislature decided to license just one operation, stipulating that this one casino could not offer rooms or meals. Hence, New Orleans appears to be protecting its existing restaurants and hotels. At the same time, it mandated that the licensee must guarantee a minimum of 18.5 percent of gross revenues or $100 million per year to the state.

The lessons for states and communities are to understand what comparative advantages exist and protect them, to determine what the market size is and not overbuild, to identify the most advantageous location(s) for gambling both in terms of capacity and minimizing impacts, and to arrive at a fair but not excessive fee and tax structure.

Social Impacts

Perhaps the most difficult and least resolved issues involved in the introduction of gambling in small communities relates to the social consequences. States deal very well with the regulatory and revenue side of gambling. They increasingly acknowledge and accept gambling for its economic value. But although there are many indications of significant social consequences, most states have elected not to address them; they simply prefer to look the other way.

Although there are many indications of significant social consequences, most states have elected not to address them

It can be argued that social services are a county and/or local government function and that states should play a limited role. Yet, if one looks at the experiences in South Dakota and Colorado, particularly in their struggle to adjust to the rapid and dramatic social changes created by the introduction of gambling, it is hard to envision a state role that steps down from the large part it played in the days of the energy boom.

In the 1970s, energy-rich states often created community impact assistance funds and siting boards, provided state credit for infrastructure bonding, initiated training programs, provided grant-writing and other technical assistance, established social programs for alcohol and other kinds of abuse, set up special programs for the children of construction workers, created formulas for revenue sharing for impacted areas, and in general, were strong advocates of the affected communities.

The survey of gambling community residents revealed similar dislocations. Daily living patterns are disrupted due to construction and increased traffic. Demand increases substantially for the limited existing services. Traditional gathering places are lost and the sense of community diminishes. Social problems begin to arise, due to inappropriate gambling behaviors. Clearly, social needs call for immediate financial outlay, as do the demands for infrastructure development—and each suffers from the same delayed revenues. And, although serious crime does not appear to be on the increase, upsurges in theft, drunken driving, public intoxication, disorderly conduct, liquor violations and disturbances have surfaced. The telephone surveys regarding state policy showed very limited state activity anywhere that addressed these dislocation and crime issues.

Such a "hands-off" policy may work if gambling is being introduced into a community with adequate physical and social infrastructure—one that can absorb the impacts from gambling. However, if gambling is being introduced into very small towns, as is the case in Colorado and to a lesser degree in South Dakota, it is totally unrealistic to think the community has the resources and wherewithal to cope with the initial variety and scale of impacts likely to occur. To limit or deny state assistance abandons not only the community: It denies the gambling industry, which is making significant investments. A hands-off policy also neglects the needs of tourists who are a substantial market for every state, and who will judge whether to return based upon their experience. Part of this assistance is simple recognition by the state that gambling is an industry.

To limit or deny state assistance abandons not only the community: It denies the gambling industry, which is making significant investments

Not all the social impacts are negative. For example, both Deadwood and the Colorado towns reported a noticeable drop in welfare payments for single parents who were unable to leave the community to seek employment but were now able to work in the gambling industry. And residents enjoy having additional restaurants, entertainment and other amenities available in town. Further, these services now are available throughout the year, not only during the summer.

At the same time, residents lament the loss of local places that are amenable to informal gatherings of residents. One of the biggest obstacles to keeping the informal gathering spots and the new amenities appears to be state and local land use policy, and the requirement that land be assessed at its highest potential use. Because most landowners within the allowed area will want to retain the right to sell their property for gambling use and make the large profits associated with such sales, it becomes virtually impossible for local retail or "mom and pop" casinos to stay in business.

It should be possible to have both. States have found ways to maintain agriculture in the midst of growing urban areas—it should be possible to accommodate property use differently in gambling towns as well.

States have found ways to maintain agriculture in the midst of growing urban areas—it should be possible to accommodate property use differently in gambling towns as well

One way to handle negative social impacts may be for towns to develop a comprehensive plan that restricts gambling to a small portion of the town or encourages its development in areas adjacent to town. Once gambling is approved for certain areas, it becomes very difficult to retroactively restrict its location. With adequate planning, the main street can retain some semblance of normal activity. Colorado and South Dakota didn't do that because they were reintroducing gambling in downtown areas that historically had offered it. However, in Deadwood, the original Costner project would have been built on the edge of town due to the space requirements for the development and the lack of available space in the downtown area.

How to Cope: Planning for Change

What all the complexity with regulation, revenues, economic development and social impacts suggests is that planning is essential at the community, state and industry levels. And such planning should start at the early conceptual stages. With the exception of Laughlin, Nevada, and perhaps a handful of other places, few areas with gambling started with a well-thought-out vision of what they wanted gambling to look like—and then implemented the controls to achieve it.

States can help local communities work through the many decisions that have to be made. They can help these communities address a wide range of inescapable questions.

Scale. One of the first sets of questions to be addressed pertains to scale.

♥ What is the carrying capacity of the geographic area that will be adopting gambling? Does it have the capacity to adapt to the changes that will take place—and to sustain its efforts? What will it take to increase that capacity?

Will the gambling area be a day-trip excursion close to metropolitan areas, or will it be an overnight destination?

♥ Will the area be a day-trip excursion close to metropolitan areas, or will it be an overnight destination? What will be needed to attract people to and accommodate them in the destination area? If day trips are most likely, how does the community manage gambling without disrupting the quality of life for the residents of the community? What else can local residents and businesses do to capture revenues from day-trip gamblers?

♥ Does the area want what Deadwood and Colorado thought they were getting: small-scale, quaint, historic gambling—a few machines to augment existing businesses? Does it want medium-scale casinos, which are simply part of a broader tourism experience where tourists recreate during the day and gamble at night? Or does the community want to embrace gambling as a full-scale entertainment industry, with new hotels, restaurants and variety entertainment?

♥ Does the state want gambling in its urban areas—which can readily absorb the impacts? Or does it want gambling in rural areas, either because of historic precedent, community need or desired distance from state population centers?

Competition. A second set of initial questions revolves around what the competition is likely to be.

♠ Is gambling likely to spread to nearby towns, Indian reservations or states?

♠ If the competition will come from reservations, can local gambling compete with the higher stakes, greater variety of games or longer hours that may be allowed by the tribe? Can the state address those factors in its compact negotiations with the tribe? Does the local area offer other amenities that may compensate for the difference?

♠ Does the state already allow other forms of gambling—such as dog or horse racing, off-site sports betting, video lottery terminals or others—that may affect or be affected by the draw from the limited-stakes enterprises?

♠ Is gambling interest showing signs of peaking? Are there other activities occurring that may cause tourists to not want to gamble in that particular site? Is the state likely to rethink its statewide gambling policy?

Who Benefits? A third set of early questions centers around who should benefit from the gambling. Revenue distribution, discussed earlier, raises additional considerations.

♣ How can states and communities capture benefits from those who may profit most—property owners who sell early for large profits and leave? Do states or communities have real estate transfer taxes available?

How can states and communities capture benefits from those who may profit most—property owners who sell early for large profits and leave

♣ How can states help locals benefit from gambling—as owners, employees, related businesses and local communities? How can considerations such as scale of operation, local training programs, local lending practices, tax structures, technical assistance and local planning and zoning be used to maintain a level playing field for locals?

♣ Does the state want to provide benefits to a region of the state, rather than just a single community? Is the state able to overcome historic rivalries between communities by providing incentives for joint efforts, ensuring revenue sharing, requiring joint applications and similar measures?

♣ Does the state want to provide or facilitate regional planning efforts, making sure to include all the relevant parties, to address concerns related to traffic, water quality, land use, tourism and recreation development, or other pressing issues?

Once these "What do we want?" questions are answered, then planning can begin in earnest

Once these "What do we want?" questions are answered, then planning can begin in earnest, using the full range of tools—zoning, other ordinances, grant programs, contracts, awards, technical assistance and reporting requirements.

If limited-stakes gambling is intended to primarily benefit residents of the local community, policymakers should ask a few other questions:

◆ How do residents generally feel about gambling? Do they support gambling in their community? Will they receive economic or social benefits from gambling?

◆ How will the town change if it has gambling? Will gambling alter the attractiveness of the community to residents and others? Will there be more congestion? More job opportunities? More opportunities for cultural exchange? Will there be changes in the level of government services? In social opportunities or preservation of history? In the local economy generally? Will property taxes increase? Will the cost of living go up? What about the quality of the natural environment? Will there be more crime?

◆ How will gambling affect residents' attitudes toward living in their community? Will it change their level of satisfaction? The degree to which they choose to be involved? Their sense of safety and security? The way they affiliate or seek rewards? Their attitude about the preservation of their community's history?

◆ How will gambling affect residents' influence on local political decisions? On city political decisions in general? On budget decisions? On decisions influencing gambling? On decisions regarding construction and use of public facilities? On how the city allocates gambling revenues to support other community services?

◆ How will residents' personal behaviors or attitudes change if gambling is approved? Will residents gamble more? Will family members gamble more? Will residents seek employment or invest in gambling?

If one word describes the experience of bringing limited-stakes casino gambling to small communities, it would be "dynamic"—lots of momentum and constantly changing.

At some point there may be enough experience with gambling to know on a systematic basis what is needed and how to respond, but that point is not here yet. Until then, the one piece of planning advice commonly heard from all constituencies that have experiences with gambling is to be ever-vigilant. Every jurisdiction reports unanticipated problems, new pressures, the need for constant monitoring and other concerns. A state can play a very helpful role, monitoring the community's ability to handle issues, the health and integrity of the industry, the value of the experience to the state's visitors, the effectiveness of service delivery to the communities, and the impacts on other parts of the state.

If one word describes the experience of bringing limited-stakes casino gambling to small communities, it would be "dynamic"—lots of momentum and constantly changing

Chapter 7. Hold 'em or Fold 'em: The Gambling Decision

The South Dakota and Colorado cases, together with the reported experiences from other states, make it apparent that gambling is "different." It is treated differently than any other economic activity.

Gambling is different because of the possibility of quick windfalls, for states as well as communities. It is different because of long-standing moral rejection and because refusing to deal with that moral rejection overtly in policy can lead to ineffective or unanticipated policy outcomes. It is different because of the potential for fraud and criminal activity if it is not carefully regulated. It is different because of the substantial change, both good and bad, that it can cause in communities.

As a first step a state ideally will decide either that it doesn't want gambling, or that it wants gambling and then take appropriate action. Perhaps the worst thing a state can do is hope the issue will go away, and then, when an initiative passes or there is pressure on the legislature because of neighboring states' gambling activities, quickly patch together a set of reactions.

The worst thing a state can do is hope the issue will go away, and then quickly patch together a set of reactions

Fold 'em

A state may decide that it wants nothing to do with gambling. Two states, Hawaii and Utah, have decided just that, and allow no form of gambling—not even a lottery or charitable gambling. More often states allow some forms, may prohibit one or two others, and are silent or inconsistent on the balance.

In the past, ill-defined policy didn't matter; but today, due to the growth in Indian gambling, a state may want to reconsider its policies. The courts have made it very clear that if a state allows any form of gambling—whether through constitution, statute, executive order or simply regulations and licensing—then it does not have a prohibition against gambling. When there is not a complete prohibition of gambling, tribes within a state may request negotiations to offer Class III gambling. (See *Indian Gaming Regulatory Act* on page 6.)

Successful negotiations by tribes may cause problems for states that don't want gambling, for at least two reasons. First, it is almost a certainty that if tribal gambling is initiated, pressure will build from non-Indians to have a "level playing field." Minnesota is one state that has a number of reservations offering gambling but has not expanded to non-Indian casinos. That appears to be more the exception than the rule, however.

Second, because states and tribes have to negotiate terms for the conduct of Indian gambling, a state will be in a better position legally if it has clear policies about gambling. Without clear guidelines, states will be in a far weaker position if tribes should take them to court over the negotiations. The outcome could be greatly expanded Indian gambling or larger tribal casinos than the state might like to see. This, too, is an area that is very much in flux. Already there are proposed amendments to the Indian Gaming Regulatory Act. Many lawsuits relative to tribal gambling and state negotiating postures are currently wending their ways through the courts.

Being Forced to the Table

A state may decide it does not want gambling, review its laws and policies so that they are in order, and then find that a citizen initiative puts gambling in place anyway. This has been a recipe for chaos.

Not only does this situation leave the state little time to do the necessary homework, but few people will be enthusiastic about making gambling work. Moreover, if a ballot initiative appears, speculation runs rampant. Real estate values soar. People panic at the potential destruction of their lifestyle. Construction and other "development" activities begin before revenues are available or planning is complete—and the gaming commission, once formed, has a ready-made lobby waiting for it. Adversarial relations at all levels almost certainly result.

Once an initiative passes, the state has little choice but to implement it as best it can. However, during the initiative campaign, the state can play a strong role in providing information. Experience is accumulating rapidly on both the pros and cons of gambling as well as on strategies for dealing with gambling in various situations. As gambling begins to stabilize nationwide, we will know better how to respond.

Experience is accumulating rapidly on both the pros and cons of gambling as well as on strategies for dealing with gambling in various situations

Hold 'em

If a state decides to allow gambling, then it should learn from this policy manual and other sources. It should try to understand everything it can about the *experience with gambling elsewhere*—how it was regulated, what the revenue trends were, what prudent uses of revenues existed and how other states worked with both the industry and the communities. States should understand what the tradeoffs were and what safety nets have been put in place.

A state should define as precisely as it can what *outcomes it is seeking*. Does it want large-scale economic development to result? Additional tourist amenities? Is it simply trying to appease a particular constituency group? Or just trying to stay even with its neighbors? Does it want to target rural or particular depressed areas or to contain gambling in urban areas? Is it simply trying to avoid cutbacks or levying new taxes? Is it prepared to deal with the inevitable moral objections? The answers to these questions are critical in providing key guidance in what state policy should look like.

The state also should try to learn everything it can about the *nature of the industry*. Profitability of casinos rests on many factors—the tax rate and level of device fees, the number of casinos operating and the number of devices within these casinos, the initial investment required, cash reserves to withstand short-term fluctuations, interest rates on investments, the type of games offered, the amount of competition from elsewhere, the cost of operations, the ability to draw customers from outside the community, and the limits on operations established by the state. Profitability is a key question for states if their policies are predicated on the assumption that the industry will be a "cash cow." As gambling opportunities become ever more available, that assumption is likely to become increasingly faulty.

States must understand and be prepared to respond to the pressures casino owners feel to expand—to offer accommodations, good food, drinks, additional kinds of games, entertainment and family activities. In general, connections to convention centers, other tourist draws and special events tend to benefit gambling. The answer to the question of which of these additions makes the most difference will vary by setting, but a state should anticipate that it will receive requests for these kind of changes.

In addition, it is likely that those who are not currently approved for gambling will want to jump on the bandwagon. While that is understandable, the possible saturation of the market, together with the changing pressures facing the industry, may mean that expansion will simply cut everyone's profits. States may want to consider ways to spread the benefits while trying to maintain a healthy industry.

*One widely anticipated and feared aspect of the "nature of the industry" may in fact **not** be happening: the link with organized crime*

One widely anticipated and feared aspect of the "nature of the industry" may in fact *not* be happening: the link with organized crime. While the potential is always there with any operation that turns over large amounts of cash, to date there is little evidence that organized crime has made inroads, or perhaps more importantly, even tried to make inroads. Large casinos have generally gone public with much closer scrutiny of operations, and smaller casinos tend not to turn over enough money to be of much interest to organized crime. Of course, states cannot be complacent about the risk, but many issues may be more important to a state's experience with gambling than just protecting against organized crime.

Finally, states may see casinos as a way to benefit local investors. That too is becoming more unlikely. Running a casino is a very competitive business. Experience in Colorado, and to a lesser extent South Dakota, is that outside interests with experience in the business— and with deeper reserves—will probably dominate. Unless state policies are targeted carefully to limit the scale of gambling so that it is primarily locals who are involved, a state should expect outside investors to be in charge. The positive aspect of outside ownership, however, is that new capital will be coming into the community and the state.

Once states have thought through what they are getting into, they will need to *plan as well as they can*, recognizing that the unexpected will probably occur. Most planning ingredients are well understood at both the state and community levels. However, classic planning depends on good information and predictable trends, neither of which may be present when gambling is initiated. Because of this uncertainty, governments can learn from experiments in other situations. Several groups have taken innovative approaches. The Northwest Power Planning Council has developed a planning model called adaptive management. The Environmental Protection Agency has started to use negotiated rulemaking. Resource agencies are moving toward ecosystem management. In highly changeable and uncertain situations, it is advisable to stay flexible and even experiment to get the desired outcomes.

The best way to guard against unwelcome outcomes is to put careful effort into deciding what is wanted, designing ways to achieve it and then watching carefully to make mid-course corrections

Controlling the outcome may in fact be one of the biggest challenges. Gambling is in a very dynamic state in this country. Lessons that are clear today are sure to change tomorrow. The best way to guard against unwelcome outcomes is to put careful effort into deciding what is wanted, designing ways to achieve it and then watching carefully to make mid-course corrections. The stakes are large: substantial public and private investments, a community's well-being and confidence in government. What gives a state a black eye over gambling may have nothing to do with a tarnished reputation from being lax in regulations.

Heads Up

Managing the implementation of casino gambling is not a game for the faint-hearted. Nor should it be a game of chance

Managing the implementation of casino gambling is not a game for the faint-hearted. Nor should it be a game of chance. It requires a fair-sized ante, a game plan and skill in playing. The rewards can be great—but so are the risks. And you have to be careful not to get addicted to it.

This guide is less a rulebook and more a lesson on how to keep your eyes open. South Dakota and Colorado, the first to "belly up to the bar" with limited-stakes casino gambling, deserve a round of applause for sharing their experiences, both good and bad. The authors hold one hope for this guide—that it help states that are dealing with or considering gambling avoid losing their shirts.

Endnotes

1. Patrick Long and Jonelle Nuckolls. 1992. "Assessing the Social Impacts of Gambling, as Perceived by Local Government and Agency Officials, on Permanent Residents of Black Hawk, Central City and Cripple Creek, Colorado." Boulder, CO: Business Research Division, University of Colorado.

2. Patrick Long and Jonelle Nuckolls. 1993. "Gilpin County Regional Planning Commission Resident Recreation and Park Survey." Boulder, CO: Business Research Division, University of Colorado.

3. Indiana approved gambling after this survey was conducted.

4. South Dakota State Law SDCL 42-7B-2.1.

5. It should be noted that when this survey was conducted, limited-stakes casino gambling had been approved in South Dakota for four years and implemented for three; in Colorado, gambling had been approved for two years and implemented for one.

6. Only selected highlights from the resident survey are provided in this publication. Additional details about the survey and findings can be secured from the authors.

7. There were 408 usable questionnaires from Deadwood, 165 from Cripple Creek, 71 from Central City, 28 from Black Hawk and 104 from Grand Lake.

8. For example, in Deadwood, 59 households completed the abbreviated version, while 408 households completed the full questionnaire.

9. Only the average responses to the questionnaire items are reported here.

10. *Colorado Labor Force Review*. February 1993. Denver: Colorado Department of Labor and Employment.

11. Michael K. Madden. 1991. "Economic and Fiscal Impacts Associated with the First Year of Gaming—Deadwood, South Dakota." Pierre: South Dakota Commission on Gaming.

12. George Will. February 8, 1993. "What is Gambling Mania Doing to American Society?" *Dallas Morning News*.

13. William R. Eadington. 1986 (13). "Impact of Casino Gambling on the Community: Comment on Pizam and Pokela." *Annals of Tourism Research*.

14. Alice Rivlin. 1992. *Reviving the American Dream*. Washington, DC: Brookings Institution.

15. I. Nelson Rose. 1993. *Gambling and the Law: 1992 Elections. Endless Field of Dreams*. Los Angeles: Whittier Law School.

Selected Resources

Canedy, Lowell and Jeffrey Zeiger. Fall 1991. "The Social, Economic, and Environmental Costs of Tourism to a Gaming Community as Perceived by Its Residents." *Journal of Travel Research.*

Clotfleter, Charles and Phillip Cook. Fall 1990. "On The Economics of State Lotteries." *Journal of Economic Perspectives.*

Colorado Division of Gaming Annual Report. 1992. Denver: Colorado Division of Gaming.

Colorado Labor Force Review. February 1993. Denver: Colorado Department of Labor and Employment.

Eadington, William R. 1986. "Impact of Casino Gambling on the Community: Comment on Pizam and Pokela." *Annals of Tourism Research.* 13:2.

Feitz, Leland. 1991. *Cripple Creek! The World's Greatest Gold Camp.* Colorado Springs: Little London Press.

Long, Patrick and Jonelle Nuckolls. 1992. "Assessing the Social Impacts of Gambling, as Perceived by Local Government and Agency Officials, on Permanent Residents of Black Hawk, Central City and Cripple Creek, Colorado." Boulder: Business Research Division, University of Colorado.

_____. 1993. "Gilpin County Regional Planning Commission Resident Recreation and Park Survey." Boulder: Business Research Division, University of Colorado.

Madden, Michael K. 1991. "Economic and Fiscal Impacts Associated with the First Year of Gaming—Deadwood, South Dakota." Pierre: South Dakota Commission on Gaming.

_____. 1992. "Economic and Fiscal Impacts Associated with Gaming in Deadwood, South Dakota." Pierre: South Dakota Commission on Gaming.

Rivlin, Alice. 1992. *Reviving the American Dream.* Washington, DC: Brookings Institution.

Rose, I. Nelson. 1993. *Gambling and the Law: 1992 Elections. Endless Field of Dreams.* Los Angeles: Whittier Law School.

South Dakota Commission on Gaming Annual Report and Gaming Abstract: Fiscal Year 1990. 1990. Pierre: South Dakota Department of Commerce and Regulation.

South Dakota Commission on Gaming Annual Report and Gaming Abstract: Fiscal Year 1992. 1992. Pierre: South Dakota Department of Commerce and Regulation.

Wallace, James. July 26, 1993. "Mushrooming Trade Has Games People Like to Play." *Seattle Post-Intelligencer.*

What Are the Facts? 1992–93 Limited Gaming Information Booklet. November 1992. Denver: Colorado Division of Gaming.

Will, George. February 8, 1993. "What Is Gambling Mania Doing to American Society?" *Dallas Morning News.*

Wolfe, Mark. 1990. "Excerpts from Executive Summary of the Comprehensive Historic Preservation Plan." Prepared for the National Trust for Historic Preservation. Deadwood, SD: City of Deadwood Department of Planning, Zoning and Historic Preservation.

Acknowledgments

The authors would like to express their appreciation to
the many people who contributed to this publication. They
include the residents and public officials of Deadwood,
South Dakota, and Black Hawk, Central City, Cripple
Creek and Grand Lake, Colorado; state agency officials
both directly and indirectly involved with gambling from
South Dakota and Colorado, as well as from the other
states that responded to our requests for information; and
the participants of our initial workshop.

We thank those who provided their critical review of
this publication: Joe Behm, Executive Director, Central
City Casino Association; Jeff Bloomberg, State's Attor-
ney, Lawrence County, South Dakota; Dr. David Edgell,
Director, Office of Policy and Planning, United States
Travel and Tourism Administration; Pam Greenberg,
Policy Specialist, National Conference of State Legisla-
tures; Don Gromer, Executive Secretary, South Dakota
Commission on Gaming; Yong-Soon Kang, Marketing
Division, University of Colorado; Tom Kitts, Communi-
cations Director, Colorado Division of Gaming; Stephanie
Lenhart, Policy Analyst, Boulder, Colorado; Blaine Liner,
Director, State Policy Program, The Urban Institute;
Jonelle Nuckolls, Tourism Research Specialist, University
of Colorado; Dr. Mark Rom, Assistant Professor of Public
Policy, The Georgetown University; John Sem, National
Cultural Tourism Program, University of Colorado; John
Sharpe, Executive Director, Cripple Creek Chamber of
Commerce; and Mark Wolfe, City Planner and Historic
Preservation Officer, Deadwood, South Dakota.

A special thank you goes to Jeff Bloomberg, Don Gromer,
Tom Kitts, Mike Matzko, Jonelle Nuckolls and Mark
Wolfe, who served as important sources of information
and insight throughout this process; to Dr. Rick Perdue
and Yong-Soon Kang, who assisted with the design and
analysis of the resident survey; and to Janet Topolsky,

Nita Congress and Dr. Mary Hale, who so diligently
edited this manuscript.

Finally, we wish to express our sincere gratitude to
the staff of the Rural Economic Policy Program of The
Aspen Institute—Meriwether Jones (Director), DeWitt
John (former Director), Janet Topolsky (Associate
Director), Nancy Stark (former Assistant Director) and
Diane Morton (Grants Administrator)—and to The
Ford Foundation and the W.K. Kellogg Foundation for
their financial support.

Of course, the opinions expressed in this publication
are those of the authors alone. Any factual misrepre-
sentation or other shortcomings are the sole responsi-
bility of the authors.

Workshop Participants

Jeff Bloomberg
  Prosecuting Attorney
  Lawrence County State's Attorney
  Deadwood, South Dakota

Rick Brown
  State Project Officer
  Colorado Department of Health
  Denver, Colorado

Joe Forrester
  Leadville 2000
  Colorado Mountain College
  Leadville, Colorado

Mark Hemmeter
  President
  Hemmeter Enterprises
  Black Hawk/Central City, Colorado

Gary Holthaus
  Director
  Center for the American West
  Boulder, Colorado

Douglas Houston
  Patrol Sergeant
  Cripple Creek Police Department
  Cripple Creek, Colorado

Jack Kirtland
  Community Development Specialist
  State Department of Local Affairs
  Denver, Colorado

Jim Kunde
  Director
  Coalition for the Improvement of
    State and Local Government
  Indianapolis, Indiana

Jeanne Nicholson
  County Nurse
  Gilpin County Nursing Services
  Central City, Colorado

Rick Perdue
  Professor of Marketing
  College of Business and
    Administration
  Boulder, Colorado

John Starkey
  Resident and Casino Employee
  Central City, Colorado

Randy Stuefen
  Associate Director
  Business Research Division
  University of South Dakota
  Vermillion, South Dakota

Randy Wheelock
  City Council Member
  Gambling Impact Committee
  Idaho Springs, Colorado

Mark Wolfe
  City Planner and Historic
    Preservation Officer
  Deadwood, South Dakota

Jeff Zeiger
  Director
  Center for the Advancement and
    Study of Tourism
  Black Hills State University
  Spearfish, South Dakota

About the Authors

Patrick Long is an Associate Professor of Marketing in the College of Business and Administration, University of Colorado at Boulder, where he specializes in tourism and recreation planning and development. As a researcher, teacher and writer for more than a decade, he has directed numerous research and service projects focusing on rural community development. He has consulted on numerous national and international tourism projects, and is currently serving as Chairman of the National Rural Tourism Foundation.

Jo Clark is Director of Programs for the Western Governors' Association (WGA) in Denver, Colorado, where her work focuses on state policy and state roles as they relate to a broad range of issues. She has directed WGA's rural development initiative, which looked at economic development strategies, community identity and integrity, and the use of institutions of higher education to provide ongoing technical assistance to rural communities. Ms. Clark also has managed WGA's tourism and recreation program.

Derek Liston is a Research Economist in the Washington, D.C. office of KPMG Peat Marwick. He served as a Special Assistant in the Office of Policy and Planning at the United States Travel and Tourism Administration, and is a former consultant and full-time policy analyst with the Denver and Washington, D.C. offices of the Western Governors' Association. He holds a graduate degree in Public Policy from The Georgetown University and received his B.A. in economics and political science from the University of Colorado at Boulder.

The authors can be reached through:

> College of Business and Administration
> Campus Box 419
> University of Colorado
> Boulder, Colorado 80309
> Phone: 303-492-2381   Fax: 303-492-5962

The Best Practices Series

How can state and local decisionmakers address the issues of competitiveness, equity and quality of life, especially in rural communities? The Best Practices Series offers a tool kit of strategic ideas, research findings, program models and policy guidelines for state policymakers and regional development practitioners. Each guidebook in the Best Practices series is prepared by a team of seasoned professionals, who draw on field experience, published analyses and structured workgroup discussions with experts from community organizations, business, government and educational institutions. The Best Practices Series is sponsored and published by the Rural Economic Policy Program of The Aspen Institute, with the financial support of the W. K. Kellogg and The Ford Foundations.

The first six volumes of the series are:

Business Finance as a Tool for Development (1992)
by Deborah H. Markley with Katharine McKee

Designing Development Strategies in Small Towns (1992)
by Glen Pulver and David Dodson

***Gearing Up for Success: Organizing a State for
Rural Development*** (1992)
by David W. Sears, John M. Redman, Richard L. Gardner
and Stephen J. Adams

Smart Firms in Small Towns (1992)
by Stuart Rosenfeld with Philip Shapira and J. Trent Williams

***Utilities and Industries: New Partnerships for
Rural Development*** (1992)
by Charles Bartsch and Diane De Vaul

***Win ♥ Lose ♠ or ♣ Draw? Gambling with America's
Small Towns*** (1994)
by Patrick Long, Jo Clark and Derek Liston

For more information about REPP or REPP publications, please write to: Rural Economic Policy Program/The Aspen Institute/1333 New Hampshire Avenue, NW/Suite 1070/ Washington, DC 20036. Or call REPP Program Assistant Diane Morton at 202/736-5804.